WAITING TO DIE

A NEAR-DEATH RESEARCHER'S
(MOSTLY HUMOROUS)
REFLECTIONS ON HIS OWN ENDGAME

KENNETH RING

Waiting to Die: A Near-Death Researcher's (Mostly Humorous) Reflections on His Own Endgame

Copyright © 2019 Kenneth Ring. All rights reserved. No part of this book may be reproduced or retransmitted in any form or by any means without the written permission of the publisher.

Published by Wheatmark®
2030 East Speedway Boulevard, Suite 106
Tucson, Arizona 85719 USA
www.wheatmark.com

ISBN: 978-1-62787-698-8 (paperback)
ISBN: 978-1-62787-689-6 (ebook)
LCCN: 2019936315

Bulk ordering discounts are available through Wheatmark, Inc.
For more information, email orders@wheatmark.com or call 1-888-934-0888.

For Raymond Moody
who made all things possible

Contents

Foreword

My dear friend Ken Ring could have as easily become a famous humorist and writer as a famous social psychologist. I first met Ken in November of 1977. My impression of him at that time was of a bright, sensitive, warm man who was full of fascinating insights into the human mind. Since then, I have come to realize how many people all over the world he has inspired and comforted.

When I published my book *Life After Life* in 1975, I had no idea that it would attract attention beyond my family and friends. What a surprise when the book quickly became an international bestseller. Within a year, I heard about a psychology professor at the University of Connecticut at Storrs who read my book. Rather than dismissing it out of hand, he actually started his own independent study of near-death experiences. To this day, I appreciate his courage and independence in emphatically confirming my own findings about the phenomenon.

I have too many warm memories of Ken Ring to relate them in this space. So I will choose one of my memories which illustrates the drift of so many of them. In 1979, I was visiting Ken in his home, when he learned that the movie *Casablanca* was to be shown on TV that night. As we watched the movie, he admitted that he had seen it many, many times. Still, I was touched by the profusion of tears I saw pouring from his eyes.

Ken Ring is smart, funny, kind-hearted, and at times, a somewhat cantankerous man. I can always count on him for an honest and usually accurate appraisal of any idea I discuss with him.

I love him and I am sure you will too when you read his always amusing and often very insightful essays in this book as Ken describes his journey on the road toward death. I'm glad to say that he is still waiting to die, but he has assured me that he will get there in the end.

Raymond Moody MD, PhD
Oxford, Alabama
January 20, 2019

Preface

One day just after I had turned 82, I said to my girlfriend, Lauren, then 76, "You know, sometimes I think I'm just waiting to die." She gave me a look. "So do I."

We both burst out laughing.

A few days later, I decided to write a humorous little piece about what it was like, at least for me, waiting to die. After I finished it, I sent it around to a few friends who seemed to get a kick out of it. So, somewhat encouraged, I then sent the piece to some friends of mine who had websites of their own on which they were kind enough to post it, which elicited more favorable responses. I seemed to have a hit on my hands, which then emboldened me to offer it to the editors of some professional journals, and they readily consented to publish it, too.

I now seemed to be on the verge of a new career as an octogenarian humorist riffing on the wayward life of a person wandering along the road toward death. More essays followed, the first few of which were again posted on some websites and accepted by journals. After that, I simply kept writing them—I was on a roll now—but didn't want to continue to pester my friends to post them.

Nevertheless, before long I was approached by a woman by the name of Lisa Smartt who was working with the famous writer on near-death experiences, Raymond Moody, the author of the bestselling book, *Life After Life,* who happened to be a longtime friend of mine. Raymond was about to start up a new kind of university, which he was planning to call The University of Heaven. The woman had got in touch with me because Raymond had wanted to invite me to become a part of his new enterprise.

"The University of Heaven!" I spluttered. What an atrocious, off-putting, risible name for whatever he had in mind. I said, "I don't think so." And suggested a better name for it might be "Woo Woo U." The woman laughed and said she was sure that Raymond, who has a great sense of humor, would be amused.

Still, she wheedled and applied the oils of blandishments liberally, trying to induce me to join the faculty of this cockamamie, so-called university. Then, finally, she said the magic words: "We can publish your essays, and they will be read by thousands of people."

Hmmm, that stopped me in my obdurate tracks and caused me to put my heretofore adamant refusal on hold. I thought, "That would actually be more people than ever read my books." "Tell me more," I said.

Well, to cut to the inevitable chase, I yielded, and before too many more months had passed, my essays began to appear, all dressed up and looking mighty fine, on the first Wednesday of every month, under the auspices of the University of Heaven. Every man has his price, especially vain authors who are on their last lap of life.

All the essays in this book were written during a period of one year from December, 2017 to the following December, culminating with my last essay, the fifteenth in this series, which I wrote on the occasion of my 83rd birthday.

Unless this book is being published posthumously or is being written by a ghost, it seems that I am still waiting to die, and so for that matter is my girlfriend. Of course, it is dramatically unsatisfying, if personally gratifying, I suppose, to find that after trudging the road toward death for all this time that I still have a way to go. But I will persevere. I'm confident I will get there in the end.

In any case, I hope you will find in reading these essays that in another sense I haven't traveled in vain. I've learned a few things along the way and, despite the infirmities of age and my sometimes wearisome complaints about my increasing decrepitude, my journey has afforded me more than a few laughs, some surprises and even at times treasured moments of joy. Maybe even a valued insight or two. I think you'll see that waiting to die can have its pleasures. And if you happen to be walking that road yourself, buck up—it ain't all that bad.

Oh, I suppose I should mention one more thing. Before I became an old man descending into desuetude, I earned my keep as a professor researching near-death experiences, which I've done for the last forty years. Still, I rather regret that you are meeting me only now at this end stage of my life. I wish you could have known me when I was in my prime! So before we begin traveling on the road toward death, I thought I would to like to give you a sense of what I was like half a lifetime ago when I was full of vim and enthusiasm, and just starting out on another journey—into the fascinating land of near-death experiences. Accordingly, we will actually begin, not last year, but back in 1978. At the beginning of my life as a near-death researcher, and not yet at the end nearing my own death.

Part I

In the Beginning

Researching Life After Life: Some Personal Reflections

Not long ago, when I was reorganizing some of my books and papers, I happened to come upon an old newsletter from forty years ago that had been edited by some then friends of mine. At the time they lived just a few miles from where I now reside, and seeing that newsletter brought back warm memories of our friendship.

But what struck me most forcibly was a little essay I had written for their publication, which was sent only to the people who were members of their organization, probably something like fifty and surely not more than a hundred. I had completely forgotten about this essay, and obviously only a relatively few people had read it at the time.

When I wrote it, I had just completed the research for my first book on NDEs, *Life at Death.* I was then deeply affected by the interviews I had conducted for the book, and in the essay I wrote about it in a very personal way. I could never, and never would, have written about my research this way in my book, but here I was still in the emotional throes of my interviews and how they had already changed my life.

I was also aware that my work had completely validated that of Raymond Moody, and for that reason, I had actually entitled my essay, *Researching Life After Life: Some Personal Reflections.* In retrospect, I find something else I hadn't been so much aware of at the time — my indebtedness to Moody's book, *Life After Life.* What if I had never come across his book? How would my life have developed without that book?? Was there ever a book that was so crucial to my life's path? So, in a very definite way, if only in hindsight, I would like this essay to be read as a kind of homage to Dr. Moody and the critical role that he and his book have played in my life.

But here's what I wrote forty years ago, when I was just at the beginning of my own journey into the world of NDEs.

Beginning in May of 1977, I spent thirteen months tracking down and interviewing persons who had come close to death. In some cases, these were persons who appeared to have suffered clinical death where there is no heartbeat or respiration; in most cases, however, the individuals I talked with had "merely" edged toward the brink of death but did not quite slip over.

Since this work was part of a research project, I had trained a staff of interviewers in the necessary procedures so that I—the busy professor—would not have to conduct all the interviews myself. After I had talked with a couple of near-death survivors, though, I saw that my life would just have to get busier: this stuff was plainly too fascinating to get it secondhand. I wound up interviewing 74 of the 102 persons who eventually comprised our sample.

Although I had been familiar with near-death experiences for some years, my interest in doing research in the area had been kindled by Raymond Moody's book, *Life After Life*. I found that, although I didn't really question the basic paradigm that he described, I was left with a lot of questions after finishing the book. How frequent were these experiences? Did it make any difference *how* one (almost) died? For example, do suicide attempts that bring one close to death engender the typical near-death experience? What role does prior religiousness play in shaping the experience? Can the changes that allegedly follow from these experiences be documented systematically and quantitatively?

So I wrote a little grant proposal and got some funds in order to answer these questions.

And thereby uncovered a source of spiritual wealth that will always sustain me.

This was not exactly what I had bargained for. But I am happy to 'share the wealth" with you. Not that it's mine or was given to me. Nor does it "belong" to those who survive near-death episodes. It's just there. It's simply that talking to these persons helped me to *see* it.

In this little article, I am not going to bother to summarize the results from this study except to say that our data fully uphold Moody's findings. Virtually every aspect of the near-death experience he delineated is to be found in our interview protocols. I have no doubt whatever that he has described an authentic phenomenon (though its interpretation is up for grabs). And others, since the publication of Moody's book, have also corroborated his findings. As far as I'm concerned, then, the basic outline of the core near-death experience, as sketched by Moody (and before him by Kübler-Ross) is now established fact.

What I want to relate to you is something of the experiential residue that has remained with me now that the interviews are finished. I doubt that much of this is going to find its way into the professional publications I shall be writing based on this research or that it will even find explicit expression in a book I am planning on near-death experiences. And yet, in some way, I feel that it represents the essential *finding* of my research: that it is "the real message" hidden within the welter of statistics and the seemingly endless interview excerpts which so far make up the bulk of the manuscript I am presently working on.

You don't forget their faces or their manner during the interview. I talked to one woman who had been close to death perhaps eight or nine times owing to an unusual respiratory problem. Once, when her life was in danger, she saw a ball of light and heard what she took to be the voice of the Lord. The voice said, "You will suffer, but the Kingdom of heaven will be yours" This woman insisted that these were the exact words, nor a paraphrase or "an impression." As with so many other incidents that were disclosed to me, this one seemed fully real. People will deny indignantly that what they experienced was a dream or an hallucination. But what I remember most vividly from this interview is how this women *looked.* She radiated peace, serenity, acceptance. She knew she didn't have long to live—that the next time could be "it." She has had many personal difficulties to contend with in her life. She lives every day as a *gift.* This was not said as an empty religious platitude. I could *see* it. She never said so, but it became clear that her friends are deeply inspired by her example. (She herself makes light of it all.) I looked at her face as she continued talking. It seemed lit up—from the inside.

How do you think I felt when I left her house?

I remember another woman. She had had her near-death experience more than twenty years ago. (Most of those we interviewed had come close to death within the past two years.) Her doctor had botched up a routine tonsillectomy and a cardiac arrest had resulted. According to the information she gave me and from what I could glean from her medical records, it appears that she was clinically dead for nearly three minutes. I'll relate just a portion of what she told me:

> ...the thing I could never—absolutely *never*—forget is that <u>absolute</u> feeling of [struggling for words] peace... joy...or something. Because I remember the <u>feeling</u>. I just remember this *absolutely beautiful feeling.* Of peace. And happy! Oh, so happy! That's about the only way I can explain it. And I was above. And there was a presence. It's the only way I can explain it because I didn't *see* anything. But there was a *presence,* and it may not have been *talking* to me, but it was like I knew what was going on between our minds. I wanted to go that way [toward the presence]. *Something* was there. And I had no fear of it. And the <u>peace</u>, the release. The fear was all gone. There was no pain, there was nothing. It was *absolutely beautiful*! I could *never* explain it in a million years. It

was a feeling that I think everyone *dreams* of someday having. Reaching a point of ABSOLUTE peace. And ever since then I've never been afraid of death.

The woman who told me all this (and much more!) is now in her mid-fifties and recently suffered a near-fatal heart attack. There was nothing about her manner that suggested she was denying the fear of death that Ernest Becker says each of us carries within us. I wish he could have met this woman! No reaction-formation here! I have seen her socially several times since. She is the same woman. Love of life and of others animates her. Well, maybe she was always like this, but she denies it. She traces this attitude to the time when she was "dead."

Suppose you had interviewed her. Suppose you had interviewed *dozens* of persons who described to you similar feelings, experiences and aftereffects. What impressions do you think you'd be left with as you drove back to the university?

Another person who made a deep impact on me was a husky-voiced, elegant woman in her late forties. At the time of my interview with her, she lived in a tasteful, well-appointed home in a well-to-do suburb of Hartford. The outward comfort of her life was in sharp contrast, however, to her years of severe physical suffering and psychological torment. Two years before I met her, she had lain, alone and comatose, in her home for three days before she was discovered and brought to a hospital. She had apparently suffered heart failure and lay close to death for a long time.

This extended period during which she hovered between life and death enabled her to have a very deep experience, perhaps the deepest of any I heard recounted. She eventually found herself surrounded by a radiant light, feeling totally peaceful and ecstatic, reunited with her deceased parents, and in an environment which can only be described as representing a vista of what most people would call heaven. At the height of her joy, however, she felt herself being pulled back by the appeals of her children who stood around her bed, and at this point remembers experiencing an agonizingly painful wrenching sensation, as though, she said, "I were being pulled out of a *tremendous vacuum* and just being torn to bits."

Before her return to life she remembers thinking:

One very, very strong feeling was that if I could *only* make them (her doctors and others) understand how comfortable and how *painless* it is, how *natural* it is. And the feeling that I had when this was happening was not that I was becoming non-existent, but that I was becoming just another identity, another part of me was being born. I don't feel that it was an ending of my personality or my being. I just felt it was another beginning of my being. I felt *no* sadness. No longing. No fear.

Even when she was feeling the pain of being caught between the worlds, her resolve did not ebb:

I cannot tell you exactly *what* happened—whether I heard my daughter or my children speak to me, and when they said, "we need you! (But) suddenly, the immensity of what I had experienced somehow made me realize that I *had* to, I *have* to make people understand. I have to make them realize that death is not a frightening or horrible end. *It is not.* I *know* it is not! It's just an extension or another beginning.

Since the time of this incident, this woman has been attempting to share her experiences with others. She has spoken to journalists, radio reporters, and was even in a film documentary that dealt with the experiences of dying. To live in accordance with what her near-death experience disclosed has become her life's aim. At the present writing, this woman is undertaking a program to counsel the dying and the sick. She has found her life's work and she found it through encountering her own death.

She is not the only person I talked with whose experiences have led to a mode of life devoted to helping others deal with their own deaths. Such persons who have had a near-death experience come to engage in this work but not simply out of a desire to do something useful or kind, but from an inner conviction that their own experience, by virtue of its having been vouchsafed to them, is *meant* to be shared so as to provide comfort and reassurance to those who are about to take their own journeys into something that we call death. And there is something about such people I have noticed, some special quality they have that draws you to them. They seem to radiate in life the peace that they felt when they were close to death. And it *does* something to you.

I could mention many other persons I talked with who have this ability to make a gift of their presence, but I think I'll relate just one more vignette. Again, it is a woman (I think I should say that I found no sex differences in incidents of near-death experiences and many men gave me deeply affecting accounts of their episodes; it just happens that the memories that come first to mind in connection with this article all involve women), but this time it is a woman who had no conscious, Moody-type experience. In fact, though she never read Moody's books, what she had heard about such purported experiences had left her feeling skeptical in the extreme.

I had driven a long way through a dreary rain to get to her home and when I rang the doorbell, there was no response. I was about to ring again when the door finally opened. A middle-aged woman, her face showing the pain which still affected her body, silently invited me inside. I understood immediately on seeing her that she could only move slowly and with difficulty. That explained the long delay on her doorstep. She lived alone. Her husband had died some years before. Her daughters, whose photographs were displayed on the living room wall, lived in nearby towns. I noticed that her daughters were strikingly beautiful. Her house was small, but tastefully furnished. Charming knickknacks and lovely flower filled-vases gave the living room a homey and cozy quality.

She sank heavily into a chair. Speaking slowly and with a German accent, she told me that a year and a half earlier, she had been severely injured in an automobile accident of which she remembers nothing. They didn't think she would live. She showed me photographs taken at the time; they were not pretty. She spoke matter-of-factly, without any sense of self-pity. She was still recovering and she was still suffering physically, but somehow she exuded a quality of repose and serene pensiveness. She began to reflect on what her experiences had taught her:

> In my opinion, there are two things in life which keep a person going, or, I should say, which are important. To me, they are the most important things. And that is *love* and *knowledge*. And what I experienced when I was in intensive care, not only once but several times, when I went out of my consciousness, was the closeness of another human being, the love I was treated with from everybody including the doctors and including the nurses and most of all, my family, my children. And I think a lot of people who are very religious or so will say they more or less experienced God, whatever God I believe in, right? And love was one of the things I felt (when) I was close to them. I got more of it than others. And I could *give* more of it, too. I felt very much loved and I felt that I loved everybody. I did not only tell one time that I loved my doctor and I still feel that way because they [she paused], they gave me life back again. I think that this is worthwhile, to love somebody, because life is the most precious thing. And I think you don't realize that before you actually almost die. (And) the more knowledge you have the better you will understand whenever anything happens to you. You will understand why certain things have to be this way and why.

> For example, a friend who was on a dying list, too, but he never believed in doctors, in nurses or anything like that. And he is *still* ill, and this is over a year now and he's still ill, very ill. Because he did not *trust* in the people,

that they can help. And [she paused again] I think that's very important that you *know* that certain people love you and not only certain people, but *most* people love other people... There may be some people, and one hears about it, that they live in hatred, but I think they don't have the knowledge that it is *so important to love* and to understand what life is all about because I think that's the main thing... that's what it is all about.

I asked her if she had felt that way before her accident:

I did, but I did not feel as strong as I do now. The accident, as bad as it was and as much as I suffered and as much as I will probably never be exactly the same as I was before, but mentally I think I grew. I grew a lot. I learned the value of life more than I did before and I actually gained by this experience. It's very important to me. That itself makes life worthwhile for me to go on and do whatever is in store for me, you know, and live to the full extent.

She grew quiet then, for even talking was an effort, and I noticed the timeless stillness that had come upon us. The illumination in the room was dim, but woman's face was again aglow with that inward light of peace and love that I had seen before in other near-death survivors. Everything in that room seemed hushed and still and suffused in beauty. Those of you who meditate or who have taken psychedelic trips will understand... and will understand how much words fail here. Everything—all meaning, all mystery, all holiness—was present in the specificity and precision and timelessness of that moment.

With a sense of wrong-doing, I finally broke the spell by asking another question. The interview continued. At the end I tried to express my thanks to her, but lamely. She thought I was thanking her for the interview.

Afterward, still feeling immensely moved, I felt that I wanted to send her something that would better express my gratitude to her. Since she had mentioned that she enjoyed listening to music, I chose a recording of Beethoven's A minor string quartet. The third movement of this quartet is sub-titled, "Heiliger Dankgesang eines Genesenden an die Gottheit" (Hymn of Thanksgiving to the Creator from a convalescent), and in view of her accident and ancestry, it seemed fitting. This quartet also had a special personal meaning for me since I had listened to it over and over at one point in my life when I had feared (mistakenly, as it turned out) that I might be seriously ill. I thought in listening to it, she would understand.

She replied by sending me a printed card of thanks with her signature. No more. Sometime later I wrote to her in order to see whether she might be interested in appearing in a documentary film on near-death experiences, but my inquiry went unanswered. I was somehow reluctant to call her. But I have never forgotten her or what she looked like when she spoke the words I quoted to you and what happened when she had finished speaking them.

I had begun this work during a time of sorrow and inward emptiness in my life. I remember feeling spiritually adrift, as if I had somehow lost my way. Suddenly, I found that I simply did not know what to *do*. Concealing my barrenness and distress, I took myself that summer to a nearby convalescent home and offered my services as "a volunteer." I was secretly hoping that some old wise person, contemplating his own imminent death, would somehow give me a clue as to *what* I was supposed to do. Mainly, I played cards with people in desperate physical straits and saw suffering all around. And our conversations were mostly about how well someone had played a hand of bridge or when the refreshments would be brought in. Philosophical ruminations on life were not in vogue.

It was while I was vainly seeking "the answer" at the convalescent home that I happened to read Moody's book.

During the thirteen months of interviewing near-death survivors, I received my answer. The professor had found his teacher at last. They were ordinary people who described, in a consistent way, an extraordinary patterning of experiences which occurs at the point of death. The effect of personally seeing this pattern gradually reveal itself over the course of these interviews is something I shall probably never adequately be able to convey. But this effect, combined with that quality of luminous serenity which many near-death survivors manifest, made me feel that I myself was undergoing an extended religious awakening.

Quite a few of my interviewees claimed or believed that during their experiences they encountered God directly or sensed His presence intuitively. It was really astonishing how often this was asserted by persons of all sorts of religious persuasions including non-believers. What to make of such statements is, of course, another matter. Professional interpreters can debate the question. As for me, I can only say that I have no doubt I saw Him, too. He left His mark on those I talked to. And they left their mark on me.

Part II

On the Road

CHAPTER ONE

Waiting to Die

The bright realization that must come before death
will be worth all the boredom of living.

—NED ROREM

What's it like, waiting to die? Of course, it's different for everyone. I can only say what it's like for me. On the whole, it's rather boring.

Don't get me wrong. I still have many pleasures in life and— knock on silicon—I'm lucky not to be suffering from any fatal illness, though if I were, that would certainly add some drama in my life. I could then follow the example of the poet Ted Rosenthal, who after contracting leukemia, joyfully called his friends and said, "Guess what's happened to *me!*" Well, no thanks. I'll take my boring life any day and intone a hymn of gratitude every morning I wake up with only the ordinary indignities of an old man—coughing, wheezing and sneezing, and, oh, my aching back!

But still….I'm used to having productive work—writing books, helping other authors with their books, being involved in various professional pursuits, and so forth. But recently I published my last book, which I puckishly entitled, *Pieces of My Mind Before I Fall to Pieces,* which was a kind of potpourri of stories and interests from my later years, and just after that I wrote what I expect to be my last professional article, the foreword to a colleague's memoir. Now what? More precisely, what do I do with my time now that I have clearly entered the epilogue of my life? Honestly, I feel as if I have stepped over the threshold into my afterlife before dying.

Of course, I can watch films—I've become quite a "film buff" in my later years; I still have interesting books to read. I am blessed with a wonderful girlfriend. Still, since life has become a spectator sport for me, and I can no longer travel, except locally, I find that I am spending more time on my sofa, honing my couch potato skills, watching sports. Yet I must confess that even they have lost a good deal of their zest for me. My home town baseball team, the San Francisco Giants, finished in the cellar last year; in golf, Tiger has gone away; in basketball, Michael Jordan is long gone; and in tennis, which is now the only sport I follow with some avidity, it is chiefly because of the great Roger Federer. Nevertheless, I can only wonder how long he can at 36 continue to produce one miracle after another. Surely, he, too, will begin his inevitable decline soon, and with his descent from the heights of glory, my interest in tennis will also flag. So what will be left then? I will tell you.

The body. Mine. It has already become my principal preoc-cupation and *bête-noire*. These days, I can't help recalling that St. Francis referred to the body as "brother ass." It seems I now spend most of my time in doctors', chiropractors' or dentists' clinics, as they strive to preserve my decaying body parts by inflicting various forms of torture on me that would even impress Torquemada, or doing physical therapy in what is most likely a vain attempt to delay the encroaching onset of wholesale physical deterioration. Really, is this any way to run a navy? There are many days when I think the only surgery that will preserve me would be a complete bodyectomy.

Well, okay, I realize this is only par for the course of the everyday life of an octogenarian. Wasn't it Bette Davis who famously said "old age is no place for sissies?" It isn't for wimps like me either, it seems. (I can often be heard crooning, "turn back the hands of time….") Still, I wouldn't go so far as the saturnine Philip Roth who said that old age is "a massacre." I guess at his point I find myself somewhere between Davis and Roth, but the waiting game still seems to be a losing proposition and I might very well come to think of my current boredom as the halcyon days of my decline.

Nevertheless, consider a typical day in the life of this old wheezing geezer.

It begins with the back. Every day does. In the morning, you get up, but your back doesn't. It hurts. Even though you take a hot shower before bed, by the time you wake up your back has decided to take the day off. When you try to use it, as for example, when you bend over to pick up the comb you've dropped into the toilet, it begins to complain.

And finally, it gets so bad, you have to lie down on your once neatly made bed, remove half your clothing, and apply some ice to it while listening to mindless music and cursing the day when some enterprising hominid decided it would be a good idea to change from the arboreal life to a bipedal one. Big mistake. The next one was the invention of agriculture, but never mind. We were talking about the back and its vicissitudes.

Nevertheless, a little later, you decide to take your body out for a spin. "Don't look back,"the great Satchel Paige advised, "something might be gaining on you." In my case, it's the man with the scythe whom I hope to outstrip for a few more years.

Of course, the back, which had only been moaning quietly before now begins to object vociferously, asking sourly, "what the hell are you thinking?" Nevertheless, you press on, thinking your will will prevail, and your back can go to hell.

But the next dispiriting thing you notice are all these chubby old ladies whizzing by you as if they are already late for their hair appointments. How humiliating—to be passed by these old biddies! You think about the days in junior high when you were a track star, setting school records in the dashes and anchoring the relay races, which you used to run in your bare feet. Then you ran like the wind. These days, you are merely winded after trudging a hundred yards.

When you can go no further, you turn around only to become aware of still another distressing sight. Actually, it *is* your sight—or lack of it. It ain't working. You could see pretty well after your corneal surgery last year, but now you can't see worth shit. What is that ahead of you? Is it a woolly mammoth, a Saint Bernard or merely a burly ex-football player? Where are the eyes of yester-year? Gone missing. Well, they didn't give me any guarantees as to how long my vision would last before it decided, like my back, to begin to object to its continued use outdoors. The way of all flesh doesn't stop with the flesh; it continues with the cornea, so now I am cursing the darkness in the middle of a miasmal morning.

I finally arrive home in a disconsolate mood, but now it is time to hop onto my stationary bike, which is the only kind I have ever been able to ride since my balance is worse than that of an elderly inebriate on New Year's Eve. I used to be able to pedal reasonably fast and for a long time. But lately someone must have snuck in to affix some kind of a brake to the bike since suddenly it seems that I am pumping uphill at an acute angle. Heart rate is up, speed is down, my old distance marks are a treasured memory, which I can only mourn. All I am aware of now is the sound of someone huffing and puffing.

At last the torture is over, but now I really have to piss. That damn enlarged prostate of mine has no patience—it must be sat-isfied *now!* I race into the bathroom, unzip my fly before it is too late, and make sure, because I have my girlfriend's admonitions in my ears as I piss that she will behead me if I continue to treat the floor as an auxiliary pissoir, I am pissing very carefully into the toilet bowl. Of course, these days, my urinary stream is a sometimes thing. It starts, it stops, it pauses to refresh itself, it pulses, stops, dribbles, starts up again with what seems to be its last mighty effort to produce something worthwhile and finally drips itself into extinction.

I'm relieved, however, because at least I haven't soiled my pants this time. But wait. What is that? Pulling up my pants, I can feel some urine on my left thigh. How the hell did it get in there? Is there some kind of silent secondary stream that runs down the side of my leg when I am otherwise preoccupied with trying to keep my penile aim from going astray?

Now I have to find a towel to wipe off the offending liquid and just hope my girlfriend won't say, when I return to the kitchen, "what is that funny smell, darling?"

Well, you get the idea. Life is no longer a bowl of cherries, or if it is, some of them are turning rotten. And naturally I can't help wondering how long I have to go before I *really* cross that final threshold over the unknown. For years, I've joked that I've wanted to live to be 1000—months—old. Now I'm at 984 and counting. I'm getting close, and it's no longer just a joke.

And of course I now also have to wonder what will be next? I mean, after I die, assuming I will ever get around to it.

Well, in my case, I have some inklings because I've spent half my life researching and writing about near-death experiences and in the course of my work I've interviewed hundreds of people who have told me what it was like for them to die—at least for a few moments—before returning to life. And what they have told me has been, I am frank to admit, profoundly reassuring.

I remember one woman who said that in order to grasp the feeling of peace that comes with death you would have to take the thousand best things that ever happened to you, multiply them by a million and *maybe,* she said (I remember her emphasis on the word, "maybe"), you could come close to that feeling. Another man said that if you were to describe the feelings of peace that accompanied death, you would have to write it in letters a mile high. All this might sound hyperbolic, but I have heard such sentiments from many near-death experiencers. Here's just one more specific quote from a man I knew very well for many years, telling me what it was like for him to die:

> It was a total immersion in light, brightness, warmth, peace, security....I just immediately went into this beautiful bright light. It's difficult to describe....Verbally, it cannot be expressed. It's something which becomes you and you become it. I could say "I was peace, I was love." I was the brightness. It was part of me....You just know. You're all-knowing—and everything is a part of you. It's just so beautiful. It was eternity. It's like I was always there and I will always be there, and my existence on earth was just a brief instant.

After listening to so many people describe what it was like for them to die, it is easy for me to imagine what it might be like for me—for anyone—to take that final journey. And many great writers have said much the same thing as those I have interviewed have told me about what is in store when we die. Walt Whitman, for example, who wrote "And I will show that nothing can happen more beautiful than death." And Herman Melville, with even more eloquence, said, "And death, which alike levels all, alike impresses all with a last revelation, which only an author from the death could adequately tell." It seems that in our own time, these authors from the death are today's near-death experiencers, and the revelations they have shared with us appear fully to support the claims of these famous 19th century American authors.

So having immersed myself in the study of near-death experiences for so many years, I'm actually looking forward to my passage when my time comes. Still, I'm not looking forward to the dying part. In that regard, I'm with Woody Allen who quipped, "I'm not afraid of death; I just don't want to be there when it happens." I just hope that all those stories I've heard about how wonderful death itself is aren't some kind of a spiritual *trompe l'oeil,* a cosmic joke played by a malevolent god. Or as that marvelously antic diarist and composer, Ned Rorem, whimsically jested, "If, after dying, I discover there is no Life After Death, will I be furious?"

Of course, when I am faced with the imminence of death, I hope I'll be able to comport myself with some equanimity, but who knows? Think of Seneca who wrote so eloquently about suicide, and then horribly botched his own. Well, naturally, I'm not planning to hasten my death by such extravagant means, though I wouldn't refuse a kind offer of a little help from my doctor friends to ease me on my way if I'm having trouble giving birth to my death. It can, after all, be a labor-intensive enterprise. I just hope I can find myself on that stairway to heaven I've heard so much about and can manage to avoid a trip in the opposite direction.

Meanwhile, when did you say Federer will be playing his next match?

CHAPTER TWO

One Flu Over the Dang Fool Test

I might have been a tad too glib when in the first installment of what clearly will be a terminal series having to do with my personal terminus, I observed that at least for me waiting to die was rather boring. [I was also too glib about writing off Tiger Woods; I guess I shoulda known better. O me of little faith…]

After this winter, I have had cause to change my mind. For a while there, I thought it might be more of a matter of life or death. I found myself thinking of the line Othello sings toward the end of Verdi's opera as he contemplates his own death: "Ecco la fine del mio camin." Colloquially, "This is the end of the line for me."

You see, I was one of the millions who caught the flu bug or, rather, it caught me. And held me tight for a while in what seemed to be its death-like grip. It was really bad for a week or ten days there—it's hard to remember how long. Even now, five weeks to the day after becoming sick, I am still hawking and spitting up gobs of sputum, and my voice now resembles that of your nearby frog. There were times when I considered whether the first piece I wrote in the series might well turn out to be my epitaph. And I admit there were moments, or really days, when I felt it didn't matter if that were the case since I was past caring whether I lived or died. La vie ou la mort, c'est la même chose.

I also thought ruefully that it is wise to be careful what you write about. Magical thinking or not, someone might be listening.

I remember not long after I had completed my research having to do with near-death experiences in the blind, I developed glaucoma, and as a result I am now virtually blind in my right eye and have since had a series of other ocular maladies. I'm just glad I didn't choose to research gonorrhea.

There are other well-known stories about people tempting the devil and then having to consort with him to their infinite regret.

For example, in 1904, Gustav Mahler was working on a song cycle called Kindertotenlieder (songs on the death of children). As it happened, this was only two weeks after the birth of his second child. The timing as well as the content of the work greatly upset Mahler's wife, Alma, who felt that the composer was tempting Providence. And sure enough, four years later, his daughter was dead of scarlet fever, devastating both him and his prescient wife.

But thinking about death, as I have often had occasion to do, both in connection with my many years of studying near-death experiences and as a result of nearing my own demise, however uncertain the date, can't help but conjure up certain images.

For the last several years, this is one that has often occurred to me. I am in a forest surrounded by comrades. We are all fighting an unknown enemy who keeps shooting at us. I see some of my comrades fall and die; others are wounded and lie bloody on the ground. I keep moving, hoping that no bullet will strike me.

And isn't this like life itself where death is the enemy whose bullets no one can dodge forever? We are in a war against death, and as we get older, more of our comrades succumb or if they don't die, they become disabled, infirm or demented. Or sometimes they barely escape themselves, as happened recently to a good friend of mine, almost exactly my age, who became ill with the flu at almost the same time I did but whose experience was far worse. Not knowing of his illness, I had written him on his birthday and expressed the hope that all was well with him. When he was again well enough to write, even though he was still not recovered, this is what he told me.

At just about the time that you are hoping that I am having a better time than you are, I am being stricken with overpowering symptoms of the same malady. I take a few sleeping pills and hit the sack, determined to ignore it. Alas, I awaken the next morning with high fever, urine-soaked bed, pounding headache, wicked aches and pains, and inability even to arise from the bed and make it to the bathroom. Off I go in an ambulance to the hospital, where they wheel me in to the ER for extended tests and treatment. Turns out that I too have the flu, but of a most severe strain. For more than a week after they get me back home I was literally bouncing off the walls, being unable to lift myself off the floor once I had arrived there, totally unable to control my urine, only semiconscious of what was happening around me, ignorant as to what day of the week it was or whether it was day or night, unable to grasp anything without dropping it, and so on.

I shuddered and almost cried when I received my friend's e-mail. There, but for the grace of God, etc. My friend survived and was able to dodge death's bullet, but I could easily have lost my beloved comrade. Death is all around us, but mostly we can pretend it isn't—except when it comes close or someone dear to us does die. Then we remember. When you get old, you have lots of such reminders.

Meanwhile, now that I've largely recovered from the flu, I have resumed some of my own preparations for death or taken measures to deal with my increasing physical limitations.

One set has to do with my vision, which although it is not yet deteriorated to a point where it is really worrying me, has declined significantly during the last year. As a result, I can now drive only locally and then just during daylight hours and have to depend more on the kindness of my girlfriend and sometimes other friends to tote me around.

My visual difficulties have also forced me to succumb to the lure of personal entertainment devices that have become so ubiquitous in the early part of the twenty-first century. In my case, I have just acquired an iPad so I can more easily read my favorite magazines and novels. I regard this as still another personal defeat and humiliation. I never wanted to become "one of those people."

And to spare my heirs the trouble, I am now in the process of giving away all my professional books and eventually my entire library. I have a large archive, too, much of which I will probably trash as I have not yet been flooded with offers from potential biographers to write my life story.

Downsizing and letting go—that's the name of the game I'm playing these days. Another means of making way for death.

Other factors—let's not go too much into those depressing details—have also made it increasingly difficult for me to travel, so I'm mostly restricted just to my locality in the Bay Area. I used to love to travel and have traveled widely, but now I have to get used to promenading around my own neighborhood --literally— as I have become something of a tottering boulevardier in my declining years. All that's missing is an elegant cane and a top hat.

Another doleful sign of the end times (mine, not the world's) is that increasingly I find myself thinking of people from my past who played an important part of my life. Actually, this isn't really a melancholy preoccupation at all. Because I often think of them with strong feelings of gratitude, as if I am in a sense saying farewell to them and thanking them, as it were, for all they have done for me. The other night, for example, in a conversation with my girlfriend about my early days as a graduate student, I spent a long time talking about my major professor, Harold H. Kelley, a distinguished social psychologist, whose personal care for and interest in me helped me survive a deep crisis of confidence not long after I arrived in graduate school. Kelley was venerated in his lifetime, not only for his important work but for his warm and caring nature. He saved my ass, and I will always be indebted to him.

Many years later, after I had become known for my work on near-death experiences, we happened to meet at a conference. He was much the same in his manner and friendliness, and I had a chance to tell him then, awkwardly, I'm sure, how much he meant to me. I still felt like his grateful student, and I was.

But I am not only thinking about the past. I am thinking about my future, too. Not here, but there. And about my father from whom I was separated at an early age and who died young. I have missed him my entire life and wonder whether I will soon be seeing him again.

Some years ago, as a result of a really bizarre set of circumstances, I happened to get a reading from a medium—the only one I have ever had—and my dad came through.

At one point I asked the medium whether she could give me any information about my father. This is what she told me. (My responses are in parentheses.)

> Well, first of all, I feel like he crosses before his time. Somehow you and he had abbreviated time together. (That's very true.) And I hear an apology for that. He apologizes to you, that's what I'm getting. To me, it's like in a way he was letting you down. This could be like he crossed without having enough time with you as father. It's like, "I'm sorry." He crossed very quickly, too. (Yes.) Was that from a heart attack? (Exactly.) OK, and there was no goodbye, correct? (That's right.) And you were much younger, right? (True.) [I was 17 when he died.] I just feel like there's an apology for that. I feel like he's saying he should have taken care of his health better. I don't feel that he's that old when he crosses at all. [He was 41, just as his career as an artist was taking off.] There's a tragedy around him. (Yes.)

After she gave me a good deal of evidential information about my father, she added this:

> It's also interesting in that he says he helps you with your work from the other side. Somehow organizes things on the other side that helps your work here, you understand? Were you—this is going to sound bizarre—OK, were you on Larry King or something? (That's amazing, yes, I was

on Larry King.) Really?? Was this like 20 years ago? [Damn close—it was in 1992, 19 years ago.] I'm getting something like, your dad helped to arrange getting you on Larry King. I was arguing with him, "What, Larry King?" I thought maybe I was getting it wrong. (So he's helping me?) And he has helped you. He's helped you for twenty years. Because he couldn't do it here physically, he's had to do it from the other side. [I always felt this and several years ago wrote a memoir about my dad whose main theme was my sense that he had been a continuing, loving and guiding presence in my life.]

Toward the end of the reading, I couldn't help asking the medium a question, which coming from me, will make you laugh:

(I'd like to know in the unlikely event of my death, will I see my father or will I have some connection to the various people you described to me?) Well, absolutely, but he's laughing at you! "You are asking me that when you already know the answer to that!" I mean, he's joking with me, and he sighs, and says [apparently tongue-in-cosmic-cheek], First, there's going to be a tunnel, and then, if you like, I'll greet you first, and then you're going to see all of us there...." It's almost like he's laughing at you, you understand.

Recently, I completed a little memoir I called *Pieces of My Mind Before I Fall to Pieces,* and at the very end, I wrote these lines, again about my father:

Throughout my life, I feel that I have been looked after and guided, not only by many friends and relatives as well as my various mentors, but by invisible agencies, not least of whom is my father, who have watched over me and protected me. A foolish man like me could not have made it through life without assistance from those tasked with looking after me from some unknowable elsewhere.

Of course, my time is limited (everyone's is, to be sure, but when you're in your early eighties, you are more aware that the sands of time are rapidly ebbing), and I'm mindful that I am now very close to my goal of living to be 1000 months old. My health, fortunately, is still tolerably good, but one never knows when the man with the scythe will show up at one's door saying, "it's time." When he comes, I trust I will be ready — ready to take my next adventure.

As I have said, I hope when that time comes, I will be seeing my father again. As it happens, I am finishing up the last stages of this book on his birthday.

Happy birthday, dad. See you soon!

CHAPTER THREE

The Great Debate: Is Death a Dead End?
The Case for the Prosecution

Of course, when you're in that in-between zone—what the Tibetans call a "bardo"—after your life is over but before you've died, you have plenty of time to think—to ruminate and to wonder what will happen to you when you finally cross that threshold and enter the house of death.

Oh, perhaps before I follow that train of thought, I guess I should clarify what I meant when I wrote that line about my life being over. Obviously, either I'm still here or a ghost is writing this. What I meant was that the really active part of my life has finished—no more love affairs, exciting adventures, extensive travels, doing research, writing books, and so forth—all the activities that I enjoyed so much during my life until recent years. Yes, I still have my quieter pleasures, as I have written, but mostly I am just waiting—waiting to die. And can't help speculating what will happen once I do.

Lately, I have been reading a little philosophy, not about life and death matters, but in doing so, it has occurred to me that so many of the world's great thinkers are professed atheists and are convinced that when we die, that's it. Poof! Death brings annihilation to our individual personalities and to all consciousness. We enter into a sleep from which we never awaken.

Let's consider this roster of the world's greatest minds who hold this view. There's Friedrich Nietzsche, of course, who became the most influential philosopher of the 19th century, albeit only after he had gone mad in 1889 while embracing a horse that was being beaten on the streets of Turin. And then there was Heidegger, commonly regarded as the greatest philosopher of the 20th century despite his unapologetic embrace of and involvement with Nazism. But let's not get distracted.

Another unabashed atheist who immediately comes to mind (at least mine) of whom you have doubtless heard is a fellow named Sigmund Freud, unquestionably one of the most influential thinkers of the 20th century. And then I immediately think of the psychoanalytically-inclined anthropologist, Ernest Becker, whose Pulitzer prize-winning book, *The Denial of Death,* I used to assign in one of my classes. Becker, incidentally, died before reaching the age of 50 and prepared for death by reading Chekhov, which I used to read to my mother before *she* died, but never mind. I seem to be digressing again, which may be my own way of denying death. Finally, we shouldn't overlook one of the most widely quoted philosophers of our own time, Woody Allen, who can be seen toting around Becker's book in his glorious smash hit, *Annie Hall*. And in another one of his top-rated films, *Hannah and Her Sisters*, his mordant character makes us laugh by reminding us that the universe is totally meaningless, which, leads him to consider becoming a Hare Krishna. Whatever works.

But let's continue our list of the world's most influential avowed atheists. No such list would be complete without mentioning the most revered and beloved scientist of our own time, the recently deceased Stephen Hawking whose incontestable genius was often compared to Einstein's. And how about another intellectual luminary, Steven Weinberg, one of the leading theoretical physicists of the present day and a Nobel Laureate to boot?

And then these days there are any number of literary heavyweights who find themselves in the atheists' camp. Just to take two whose books I have recently read, there's Phillip Roth whose almost vicious attacks on religion are well known as is his disdain for anyone who believes in the poppycock of an afterlife. And then just last night, I came across this passage from the English writer, Julian Barnes, when reading his almost unbearably affecting memoir concerning the death of his wife: "When we killed—or exiled—God, we also killed ourselves. Did we notice that sufficiently at the time? No God, no afterlife, no us. We were right to kill Him, of course, this long-standing imaginary friend of ours, And we weren't going to get an afterlife anyway."

To conclude our roster of prominent religious debunkers, of course we can't overlook that contemporary clutch of infamous atheists—a quartet that includes Richard Dawkins, Daniel Dennett, Christopher Hitchens and Sam Harris—no intellectual slouches, these guys.

Well, when you consider the collective brain power and enormous influence of these men—and of course they are all men (make of that what you will), the idea that death is not a dead end seems patently ludicrous—a childish fantasy for people who can't deal with the obvious fact that death brings only extinction. We like to imagine what most religions teach—that we will continue to exist even after death, but in light of all reason, this is pure balderdash.

Still, as we know, most people don't believe this is balderdash. Surveys consistently show that the vast majority of people, certainly in the United States, believe in some form of life after death. Also arrayed against the view of the intellectual giants I've mentioned is the testimony of literally thousands of near-death experiencers who have at least entered into the first stages of death, which so far as I know, none of the formidable thinkers cited above ever did before their deaths; that is, none of them is known to have had an NDE. I can only wonder if they had, whether they would have remained so sure of their position. In my research on NDEs, I can say that I have encountered more than a few former atheists who changed their mind after having had an NDE.

However that may be, almost all near-death experiencers become undeniably convinced that some form of postmortem existence awaits us all. Let me take just a few moments to offer some illustrative examples from those persons who have come the closest to crossing the bourne from which Shakespeare taught—wrongly, as it turns out—no traveler returns.

> I was standing in a mist and I knew immediately that I had died. And I was so happy that I had died but I was still alive. And I can't tell you how I felt. It was, "Oh, God, I'm dead, but I'm here. I'm me. And I started pouring out these enormous feelings of gratitude because I still existed and yet I knew perfectly well that I had died.

> I *know* there is life after death. Nobody can shake my belief. I have no doubt—it's peaceful and nothing to be feared. I don't know what's beyond what I experienced, but it's plenty for me. I only know that death is not to be feared, only dying.

> Upon entering that Light…the atmosphere, the energy, it's total pure energy, it's total knowledge, it's total love—everything about it is definitely the afterlife if you will… As a result of that [experience] I have little apprehension about dying my natural death…because if death is anything like what I experienced, it's gotta be the most wonderful thing to look forward to, absolutely the most wonderful thing.

> It gave me an answer to what I think everyone must wonder about at one time or another in this life. Yes, there is an afterlife! More beautiful than anything you can begin to imagine. Once you know it, there is nothing that can equal it. You just know!

What is striking about these quotes—and the literature on NDEs is replete with them—is not merely their unanimity of opinion, but the tone of absolute certitude that pervades them.

Those who have left their bodies behind, even for a moment, know without a scintilla of doubt that they will continue to exist, as themselves, in another world of indescribable radiant beauty.

So where does that leave us? We have two diametrically opposed points of view to consider—that of the renowned and world famous intellectual atheists I've cited and that of the thousands of unknown ordinary persons who have had NDEs. Take yer choice.

For atheists, however, the road stops here, and there is nothing further to add. But the testimony of NDEs tells us that there is something more that awaits us after death, even if they can't tell us what. The question is, is there a way to know, and, secondly, does it make sense to try to conceive of it while we are, like me, waiting to die?

The distinguished psychiatrist Carl Jung, who himself had a profound NDE when he was nearly seventy years old, was an ardent proponent of precisely this kind of imaginative exercise. In his captivating memoir, *Memories, Dreams, Reflections,* written toward the end of his life, he exhorts his readers as follows: "A man should be able to say he has done his best to form a conception of life after death, or to create some image of it—even if he must confess his failure. Not to have done so is a vital loss."

At the risk of disagreeing with the great man, I demur. In fact, I think it is a friggin' waste of time. I give several reasons for taking this position in my book, *Lessons from the Light,* but the one I would emphasize here is two-fold. First, of all, it is impossible to know what, if anything, is going to happen to us, and second, near-death experiencers themselves tend to shy away from these speculations, often implying that the world beyond death completely defies representation in ordinary language. After all, if such a task could daunt even a sublime poet like Dante, what could we expect from mere mortals when they try to describe their encounter with the ineffable?

But there is a third reason as well. Thinking about the afterlife, assuming it exists, which honesty compels us to admit we can't know for certain in any case, keeps us from paying attention to our lives here, which is the *only* thing we *can* be certain of. Didn't Ram Dass remind us, in the title of his seminal book of wisdom, *Be Here Now*?

When the time comes for us to die, either we'll find out or we won't. Why waste time thinking about it now? I'm with Omar Khayyam on this one. The hell with it. I'm going to the movies with my girlfriend. Afterward, we'll have our bread, cheese and wine, though probably in our case we'll substitute some chocolate confection for the wine. I'm alive now and, while I'm waiting to die, by jingo, I'm going to enjoy myself as long as I can.

CHAPTER FOUR

Laughing at Death

Nature has symbols for her nobler joys,
Her nobler sorrows. Who had dared foretell
That only man, by some sad mockery,
Should learn to laugh who learns that he must die?

—WILFRID SCAWEN BLUNT

I am thankful for laughter,
except when milk comes out of my nose.

—WOODY ALLEN

Not long ago, a good friend of mine, about twenty years my junior, wrote to me saying that he was already fretting about getting older:

> I have been thinking of you off and on again these days, pondering whether I should take you as my role model for how to deal with getting older. I am 61 now and quite often annoyed about the symptoms of getting older, while you often wrote things like: "There is still a lot I can be grateful for" and other encouraging things.

"Ah, my early sixties," I thought wistfully, "I was in my prime then." Well, all right, I was exaggerating, of course.

Sub-prime was more like it, I suppose, but nevertheless for

me, in retrospect, during that period of my life I was still at the top of my game, as I wrote to my friend:

> Getting older is hard, and I don't know exactly or even vaguely what's going on in your life now, but my sixties were one of my best decades—and, hopefully, it can be one for you, too. I am certainly not anyone's role model for anything, but in my view, it helps to be grateful for every small blessing, to be patient (not my strong suit) in times of adversity, and to have compassion for oneself, no matter what the circumstances. There is really only one problem—the refusal to accept what is. We all have this problem, of course. Living in a body, especially when one is older, can be a struggle, a drag, and often painful. That's life. What has helped me is trying to have a sense of humor about it and trying, hard as it is, not to take oneself or one's troubles too seriously.

Indeed, the older I've become, the more important having a sense of humor has been to me in dealing, not only with the indignities of aging, but just as much with the prospect that death itself may be just around the corner. In fact, in my last book (in surely a double sense), which I whimsically entitled *Confessions of a Humorist Manqué,* I finally decided to give voice to my humorist side that now seemed to be seeking some form of expression before it was too late to express anything at all. And at the same time, I also drew on my tribal origins in admittedly a somewhat antic fashion. Here's a slightly edited version of how it began:

> Jews are funny.
> I am a Jew.
> Ergo: I am funny.

> Well, I may be funny, but I also know that's a slippery syllogism, or as we used to say behind our teacher's back, a sillygism. After all, it doesn't say All Jews are funny. I

could be the rare exception. By the time you finish this book, assuming you get past this introduction, you can render your verdict.

But consider my background. I am old enough to have grown up listening to Jewish comics on the radio. (Do you remember radios or at least remember hearing about them? They were very popular in my day along with slide rules.) Jack Benny, George Burns and Gracie Allen, for example, and Groucho Marx, of course, or in the early days of television, Milton Berle (Uncle Milty!), Sid Caesar, Amos 'n Andy. (All right, they weren't all Jewish.) Most kids grow up wishing they could be football quarterbacks or well-healed thugs wearing shades and Armani suits. Me? I grew up wishing I could be Woody Allen, only better looking.

Anyway, when I was a kid, I had a reputation for being the quickest quipper in the West. For a while, some people even thought I had Tourette's. But no such luck. Besides, I soon found that being King of the Yock Hill didn't get you the girls. They just tended to look at you pityingly and then went for the nearest jock. So I was obliged to recess my tongue and devote it to licking the crumbs off my bagels.

Nevertheless, in high school I retained enough of my humor to be voted "class wit." (This is true. I still have my plaque. That is not true.) These days, of course, as I decline into the early stages of dementia, people tend to refer to me as a halfwit (okay, I know that's a lame joke, but what do you expect from a lamebrain?) But I think it's in the genes, anyway, because my son, Dave, recently told me that in high school, he was voted "class clown." It runs in the family, I tell you, it's tribal, it's tradition! (Think Tevye.)

[In fact, although Jews constitute only about 2.5% of the American population, they account for about 70% of comedians.]

Speaking seriously for a moment (I promise it won't last), in my life as a professor and author, I have spent much of it writing books about seemingly grim and morbid subjects, such as what it's like to die (it's not as bad as you think) or what it's like to be a Palestinian living in Israel or the West Bank (it's as bad as you think) — books that I hoped would educate and edify my readers, maybe even enthrall them if they were to read about what people actually do report when they come close to death, but don't get around to it. But I have never written a book like this one whose main purpose is to entertain. But if not now, when?

I mean, in this dark and dysphoric age in the reign of Donald I, when the world seems to be going to hell, anyway, maybe what we need is not love, more love, but laughter, more laughter. At least in the gathering shadows of our time, it is one way to keep our sunny side, up, up, before we go back to putting our heads in the sand or spending our time looking to join the local opioid club.

It also helps in dealing with aging, and, as I will illustrate shortly, even more when one is facing imminent death. But first, this is what I also sent to my sixty-one-year old friend who was kvetching about aging:

Ken's Rules for Aging (and Living)

1. Aging is a myth and death is an illusion; relax.
2. Don't gripe about the things you can't do; just be grateful for those you still can, such as breathing.
3. Kvetching is okay, but try not to whine; it is unbecoming.

4. Get off your duff; sitting conduces to decay.
5. Don't act your age; there is no merit in it.
6. Enjoy life; why do you think you're here?
7. Don't worry about the woes of the world; there is nothing you can do about them.
8. Be kind to animals and occasionally to people.
9. Smile when you greet strangers; it might just buck them up and bring them out of the dumps.
10. Touch people if they let you, and hug them if you can.
11. Practice non-random acts of sexuality.
    11a. You're never too old to make love; you just may have to figure out new ways to do it.
12. Eat as much dark chocolate as possible (but don't overdo it).
13. Most important: Don't forget to love yourself and spread your love to others.
14. Don't fret about following these rules; we are all human, especially you.

But in these essays, we are mostly concerned not with aging as such, but with living in the shadow of approaching death. Here, too, however, humor in the face of death, even especially of imminent death, is perhaps the best way, literally, to have the last laugh.

Consider, for example, these humorous *bon mots* from some famous people who were about to die:

The French poet, Paul Verlaine, when he heard a friend whisper, "he is dying," said: "Don't sole the dead man's shoes yet."

Another famous poet, also famous for his prodigious drinking, Dylan Thomas, said: "I've had eighteen whiskeys. I think that's the record."

The novelist, W. Somerset Maugham: "Dying is a very dull, dreary affair. And my advice to you is to have nothing whatever to do with it."

The Hollywood impresario, Wilson Mizner, to his doctor:

"Well, doc, I guess this is the main event!" And then to

a priest: "Why should I talk to you? I've just been talking to your boss."

I've culled these examples from a delightful little book called *Famous Last Words and Tombstone Humor* by Gyles Brandreth.

But my prime example of how to deal with imminent death with humor and cheerfulness comes from the great Scottish philosopher and historian, David Hume. Hume, during his lifetime, was well known for his anti-religious views and, like that list of famous atheists I cited in an earlier installment of this series, his atheism led him to be convinced that the idea of a personal afterlife was pure poppycock. No religious consolation for this man as he approached death, only his robust cheerfulness and unquenchable sense of humor.

There are many testimonies to this effect at this end point in his life, including one from his great good friend, Adam Smith, but here I will quote somewhat extensively from an account left to us by his literary executor, William Strahan who was with him toward the very end of Hume's life:

> His symptoms, however, soon returned with their usual violence, and from that moment he gave up all thoughts of recovery, but submitted with the utmost cheerfulness, and the most perfect complacency and resignation. Upon his return to Edinburgh, though he found himself much weaker, yet his cheerfulness never abated and he continued to divert himself, as usual, with correcting his own works for a new edition, with reading books of amusement, with the conversation of his friends; and, sometimes in the evening, with a party at his favourite game of whist. His cheerfulness was so great, and his conversation and amusements run so much in their usual strain, that, notwithstanding all bad symptoms, many people could not believe he was dying. 'I shall tell your friend, Colonel Edmondstone,' said Doctor Dundas to him one day, 'that I left you much better, and in a fair way of recovery.' 'Doctor,' said he, 'as I believe you would

not choose to tell anything but the truth, you had better tell him that I am dying as fast as my enemies, if I have any, could wish, and as easily and cheerfully as my best friends could desire.' …

Strahan also mentions at length a conversation he had with Hume in which the latter made a number of amusing remarks about an imagined encounter with Charon, the mythical Greek fellow who is charged to ferry the dead across the river Styx to Hades. At the end of these witty remarks, Hume said:

Have a little patience, good Charon. I have been endeavouring to open the eyes of the public. If I live a few years longer, I may have the satisfaction of seeing the downfall of some of the prevailing systems of superstition." But Charon would then lose all temper and decency. "You loitering rogue, that will not happen these many hundred years. Do you fancy I will grant you a lease for so long a term? Get into the boat this instant, you lazy loitering rogue.

What a wonder and wonderful man was David Hume who provides such an impressive example of how to go about dying! Of course, our circumstances as well as our characters may prevent us from emulating him when our time comes, but I can only hope when I am no longer waiting to die but am about to, I will be able to be as cheerful and good-humored as Hume was.

But unlike Hume, who did not have the advantage of knowing anything about modern research into near-death experiences, when I go to my death, I will go convinced that my end will not result in my personal extinction but in my absorption into the world radiant Light and all-encompassing unconditional love that so many near-death experiencers have encountered when they pass temporarily into the realm beyond this life. And in entering into that realm, they often report being greeted by what Raymond Moody called in his ground-breaking book on NDEs, *Life After Life,*"a being a light." It is often this being who helps the individual to review his or her life. And, guess what, even here, humor can be present.

In fact, it was Moody who first drew our attention to this surprising facet of NDEs. Here's just one small snippet to illustrate this point from one of the persons Moody interviewed for his book:

> Now, I think that the voice that was talking to me actually realized that I wasn't ready to die. You know, it was just kind of testing me more than anything else. Yet, from the moment the light spoke to me, I felt really good—secure and loved. The love which came from it is just unimaginable, indescribable. It was a fun person to be with! And it had a sense of humor, too—definitely!

I think David Hume would have felt quite at home there, after getting over his initial surprise, don't you?

In my own work, at least in my lectures an classes, if not always in my books on NDEs, I have also tried to strike a humorous tone at times in order to suggest that death, too, can have its funny side. One way I've sometimes done this is by concluding my lectures with a song I once wrote, "The NDE Blues."

Since I had a pretty good singing voice for most of my life (though now I can only croon), I would warble it on all solemn near-death occasions, such as at our meetings of our NDE organization, The International Association for Near-Death Studies (IANDS). Or at the end of my NDE course at the university. Sometimes I would impulsively sing it at conferences at the end of one of my talks. In Prague, at a big international transpersonal psychology conference, I sang it before an audience of 1500 people and got a standing ovation. Another time, visiting Elisabeth Kubler-Ross at her farm in Virginia, I sang it to her; she was amused. And once when I met the famous American folk singer, Pete Seeger, I sang it to him; he looked blank — didn't understand what the hell it was about, I guess.

It's sung to the old Gene Autry theme song, "Back in the Saddle," and here are the words. Try it.

I'm out of my body at last
Seein' my future and my past
Floating through tunnel now,
I look around say, "oh wow!"
It's so peaceful here,
I don't feel no kind of fear."
Just driftin' and singin' my song
Oh Lord, why's this tunnel so long?
But what's that ahead of me?
Is that a golden light I see?
The face of God shines through
And I'm headin' straight for you
(In a basso profundo, as befits God)
My son, you have much work to do
And your family and friends need you, too
So I'm sending you back
One more chance to get on track
You'll come to me later
(Ritardando) On my cosmic elevator
(In a natural but awed voice)
I'm back in my body again,
Wonderin' what happened just then
Was that the Lord above
Did I just imagine all that love?
I reckon I'll know one day for sure
(Ritardando) I reckon I'll know one day for sure
[Da-dum (dominant-tonic) on the guitar....]

Finally, to conclude this foray into how we can use humor to defuse the fear of death, I'd like quote a little spoof I wrote up a few years ago that perhaps I should have entitled "A Change of Heart," but I just called it Metamorphosis. It's not really about an NDE as such, but about another kind of experience that leads to a similar transformation in outlook. It concerns a certain well-known politician who was then very much in the news, but you will certainly remember him. Here it is....

One morning, two days after his heart transplant operation, Dick Cheney awoke from a pleasant dream feeling distinctly odd. For one thing, he was smiling.

His daughter, Mary, also noticed that there was something strange about her father.

She calls it to the attention of her mother.

"Mom, there is something distinctly odd about dad this morning."

"What do you mean," Lynne asks, looking puzzled.

"Well, for one thing, you know how dad always looks dour in the morning, as if life is a pain and why does he have to bother being pleasant."

"Well, that's just your father, darling."

"I know that, mom. But this is different. Dad looked positively *radiant* this morning."

"Hmm, that *is* distinctly odd," Lynne agrees.

"But that's not all," Mary continues. "What *really* was strange was what he was saying."

"Mary, I'm in a hurry this morning. You know how angry your father gets when I don't have his eggs ready for him. Please get to the point."

"OK, mom, it was about Obama."

"So?"

"He likes him now."

"*What!*"

"He likes him. He thinks he's been wrong about him all this time."

"Mary, I have no time for jokes. Now, really, I have to get to the kitchen."

"I'm not kidding, mom. If you don't believe me, ask him yourself."

"Dick, how are you feeling this morning, dear?"

"Couldn't be better." (Beaming) "I'm a new man!"

"You look well, dear. I even notice that snarl — er, I mean, that little mouth tic of yours is absent today. Ah, Dick, I was wondering—Mary said you were talking about Obama this morning."

"Yes, I've been thinking a lot about him lately. You know, Lynne, I really think I've misjudged the man. I mean, he's not such a bad fellow. And, you know something else, Biden was right. For a black man, he is very clean and uncommonly articulate. You gotta give him that."

"Dick, what are you saying!"

"I dunno, Lynne, it's just something that I *feel*. I think when I'm up and about we should invite him and Michelle over for dinner. Maybe we can make amends."

"Dick, I'm calling your cardiologist. I think the drugs that they've given you to prevent rejection must be making you delusional. I'm worried about you, honey. You're not yourself."

"Balderdash, Lynne, I haven't felt this well and this clear-headed in years. It's like I've just woken up from a bad dream—except my dreams this morning were very pleasant."

Mrs. Cheney looks ashen-faced.

"And another thing," Cheney says. "This thing about Mary, you know, her…."

"Please don't bring *that* up, Dick."

"No, really, Lynne. I'm proud she's gay, and I've also been thinking she's right about same-sex marriage. I don't know what I was thinking before. I must have been bamboozled by all those rightwing nuts and those Tea Party crazies."

"Dick, those are your people. How could you be talking this way!"

Cheney continues to beam. His mind is elsewhere, a beatific smile of satisfaction on his face.

"Doctor, I need to talk with you." Mrs. Cheney is talking on the phone, which she cannot hold steadily. Her hand is shaking too much.

"*Of course,* it's about Dick. Doctor, he is talking gibberish this morning. I mean, he is actually talking like a Democrat!"

"You don't think it's the drugs? But what else could it be?"

Mrs. Cheney pauses, and then she has an idea.

"Doctor, I know we are not supposed to know the identity of Dick's donor, but do you think…."

There is a long pause.

"I know it is against the rules, but doctor, this is the Vice-President we are talking about, and he is a very sick man, and I don't mean just physically!"

"All right, I'll wait…."

A few minutes pass. Mrs. Cheney is very agitated.

The doctor comes back on the phone.

Mrs. Cheney listens with stupefaction.

Then she faints.

Mary, hearing a noise, rushes in, sees that her mother has now staggered to her feet and is sitting, dazed, in a chair, her eyes glassy.

She picks up the phone.

"A teen-aged *black boy.* From Chicago?"

Do you think I might have a future as a satirist while waiting to die?

CHAPTER FIVE

Goodbye to All That

What is the bane of an old man's life? That's obvious. Naturally, it is the body. But what is the bane of an old professor's life? (No fair peeking ahead!)

Give up? I will tell you.

It's his archive. Oy, what troubles it has caused me during this time of waiting for the end to come. Rumor has it that I will perish, but meanwhile I have been consumed with the effort to make sure that my archive survives my death. It's paper immortality I am going for.

Let's start at the beginning. What is an archive? In my case, it's all the professional crap I had accumulated during my forty or so years as a professor and author that I had felt worth preserving in hopes that one day an enterprising biographer would find his or her delight in trawling through it. (If there are any takers out there, get in touch. I'm taking applications.) The contents of my particular archive consist mainly of records of my research, interview tapes with near-death experiencers, reprints of articles I've written, original copies of some of my books on NDEs, lecture and workshop notes, files of all the professional presentations I've given, professional correspondence, and tons of letters I've received from people of all sorts, mostly describing various kinds of unusual experiences they have had. In short, the paper trail of my life as a professor, researcher and author in 55 boxes, give or take a few.

But the story of how I came to accumulate those 55 boxes is the sorry saga I must now relate.

When I was ready to retire from the University of Connecticut toward the end of 1996, prior to my return to California, I had to jettison a lot of my professional holdings. At the university, I had three offices at my disposal and lived in a house that could also accommodate many of my books. But I was now going to be moving into a small house. So I had a fire sale, so to speak. I gave away most of my professional books and I trashed a lot of materials I was glad to dispose of. But I still had a considerable amount of professional items I wanted to save.

What to do? I simply didn't have room for all of it, but my problem was saved by an angel.

His name was Terry (not his real name) and he was a medical doctor interested in NDEs, a colleague of mine, but hardly a friend, who happened to be there at the time I was stewing about what to do with all my stuff.

"Ken," he said, "I'd be happy to help." Terry told me simply to box up all the materials I didn't have room for but wanted to preserve. He offered to have them all shipped *at his expense* to his home in Tacoma where he'd be happy to store them in a temporary archive for however long was necessary. What a mensch! I couldn't believe my good fortune and Terry's willing to spend one of his own in order to become the custodian of these professional effects. We'll come back to Terry later.

Over the course of the next ten years or so, I added to my archive in California, and by then I had accumulated enough material to fill 30 Bankers Boxes, which I kept secure in my storage room. And there they sat—until I began to fret about what to do with them and all the boxes Terry (now in Louisiana) still had. Realizing that it was probable I would not live forever (at least not here), I knew I had to find an ultimate resting place for the entirely of my archive. But who would handle all this for me and where would it go?

You know how sometimes "the universe" works in mysterious ways to answer your unspoken prayers? Well, sure enough, another angel was soon to appear in my life who would solve everything.

Last year, I was contacted by a very distinguished psychiatrist I'll call Heinz with whom I had had cordial relations for many years. He told me that he was planning to create an archive for some of the pioneers in our field, and was inviting me to become a part of it. Of course, I was both honored and thrilled. This would certainly solve my problem. Heinz told me that a fellow named David was handling all the details and would be in touch soon to take charge of my archive.

When David showed up a few days later, he turned out to be a tall well-built fellow, seemingly in his late 30s (but actually much older than he appeared). He was extremely affable and I immediately took a shine to him, especially when he told me that Heinz had a large dedicated storage facility where my entire archive—along with the archives of others in my field—could be stored in perpetuity. And at no expense to me. Wow! I couldn't believe my luck. And more—David turned out to be some kind of computer genius and told me he had invented a digitizing procedure which would enable him to easily digitize large portions of my archive. Double wow.

He told me he would be happy to handle everything. He would first take all of my boxes and bring them to Heinz's house for an initial inventory after which they would be moved to Heinz's facility. Several days later, David showed up with a truck, and loaded all my boxes onto it, and off they went to Heinz's basement.

Meanwhile, I made contact with Terry, who had wound up taking care of that portion of my archive for twenty-two years, and told him to repack everything and have it all shipped out to David at Heinz's house. About a month later, it had all arrived. Set me back 2000 bucks, but it was worth it to have my entire archive reassembled in one place. David assured me that all was well.

But it wasn't. It couldn't have been worse.

What had happened? It turned out that for some time David had felt that Heinz had not followed through on various promises he had made regarding payment for his many services. And there were other contentious issues that flared up when Heinz returned from his travels abroad. These quickly escalated and all of a sudden—an explosion. In a fury, David was booted out of the Heinz's house and threatened with arrest if he returned. David, without resources or friends, was forced for a time to sleep in his car, and finally left the area altogether.

And left me holding the bag. I now had a big mess on my hands. *La maladizione*—the curse of the archive! It was all too good to be true. Alas, and well-a-day. Is it any surprise that not long after this fiasco, I came down with the flu and was sidelined for nearly two months?

Anyway, when I finally recovered, I had to get up to Heinz's house to inspect the damage, so to speak, and figure out what to do with my archive now. Trouble was, Heinz's house is located in a largely inaccessible redoubt and it requires a veritable Sherpa to get up there. Fortunately, I knew one who knew the way, and not long ago, she drove me up there.

There's another strange thing about Heinz's house. It was apparently designed by Escher because in order to get into the basement where all my stuff had been stored, you had to take a perilous death-defying journey down steep stairways that seemed to end abruptly, and then somehow there were a series of rickety stairs that eventually led to the outside where I was forced to surmount more obstacles before arriving at an outside padlocked door that led into the basement.

Now, you may think I'm making this up, but I'm not. I was then actually given a miners hat with a lamp attached and told to turn it on. The door creaked open and we entered into what seemed to be a coal mine. It was dark, dank, damp and eerily Dantean. I'm an old guy with bad balance and very poor eyesight. I could scarcely see anything, but imagined all manner of rodents must be loitering about, to say nothing of spiders and probably the odd snake. (All right, I'm engaging in a bit of hyperbole here, but it was indeed a spooky place.) I could finally see that my Bankers Boxes had been neatly stacked by David, but all of Terry's were sealed and only dimly visible. Obviously, there was no way that I could open them there to inspect their contents, which I hadn't seen in twenty-two years.

But I was told by Heinz's secretary (Heinz himself was out of the country again) that I had to get all it all out of there. Heinz could no longer be responsible for it, and it turned out (gasp!) that he didn't have the storage facility I had been promised in good faith, I'm sure, by David. Screwed!

Well, there's no point in dragging this out. Eventually, my Bankers Boxes were brought back to my storage room where my girlfriend Lauren and I had to inspect them, label them, and then stack them again, just as they had been before David had carted them away. Lauren, providentially, has an abandoned art studio on her property in Piedmont—across the Bay from where I live—and she said I could have Terry's portion of my archive deposited there for the time being where we could again inventory, label and stack. We did that just last week. Actually, I did the inventorying, but Lauren labeled everything in her exquisite hand, and then stacked them all since I have a bad back and am weak of limb whereas she is strong like bull, though fortunately she doesn't resemble one.

Oy, what a megillah! Perhaps now you can understand why I say that an old professor's archive can be his bane, besides being a pain in the tuchis, and a drain on his wallet.

In any case, rummaging through those boxes whose contents I hadn't seen in so long, I felt, once again, that I was saying goodbye to all that. A good part of my professional life was in those files and papers, and I felt nostalgic while sorting through them. But just as I got to the second to last box, I found a surprise, which thrilled me—a cache of about a hundred personal letters I had saved of which I had no recollection whatever. I quickly perused them, but decided to wait until I returned home in order to examine them more thoroughly to see just whose letters I had saved.

What I found was that the letters came from two periods—1975/76 and 1981/82. They included a batch of letters from my mother, one of which described a dreadful quarrel between her and my stepfather, and another set of letters from my daughter,

Kathryn, then 18, just after she had left home in Connecticut to move to Denver where she was to attend a technical school that eventually led to her becoming a master mechanic for Volkswagen. There were several antic and whimsical letters from a former student of mine turned porn star—the Stormy Daniels of her day—and some from a TV journalist named Aviva with whom I had had some riotous adventures in LA back in the day. I remember once proposing to marry her because, if she accepted, her name would have become Aviva Diamond Ring. Alas, she declined. I was, however, amused to find in one her letters several good quips from Woody Allen, one of which I could have used as a epigraph to one of these waiting to die essays. It went like this: "It's impossible to experience your own death objectively and still carry a tune."

I especially treasured a set of three letters from a professor with whom I had been very close friends when we were both teaching at the University of Connecticut. After three years, however, he took a position at the University of North Carolina. However, we saw each other again in California when I was on sabbatical leave in Berkeley in 1969 on which occasion something very traumatic had happened to him. Fortunately, he's still alive and I was able to make contact with him. He was thrilled to learn about his letters, and told me about the aftermath of that incident that had freaked him out from which he was a long time recovering. Through e-mail we renewed our friendship and since he has family near where I live, it's likely that we will be able to see each other again after all these years.

Another important discovery involved a batch of letters from a woman who had been a good friend of mine when we both lived back east. However, we had long since lost touch with each other, even though I knew she lived in California. We, too, have enjoyed reconnecting through e-mail, but what was particularly rewarding about that contact was learning that my friend, whose name is Ronna Kabatznick, had written an extraordinarily compelling book about her personal experiences while in Thailand when the Indian Ocean tsunami struck the day after Christmas in

2004. Her memoir, a beautifully crafted account of an unimag-
inably horrific catastrophe, moved me greatly and filled me with
admiration for the courage and grit my old friend manifested in
coping with that disaster. Her book, which I highly recommend,
is entitled *Who By Water: Reflections of a Tsunami Psychologist.*

There were also some very loving and indeed passionate
letters from women who were in love with me and in a couple
of cases had even moved to Storrs, where I lived, against my
express wishes. But the set of letters that really affected me, as I
re-read them, was from a woman I had loved deeply against my
will and who had almost ruined my life because of the intensity
of her love for me. I had completely forgotten about these letters
of which there were sixteen, almost all handwritten (these were
the days before computers, of course, when people still wrote
by hand). Re-reading them the other night I was struck by their
ardor, their longing, their anguish, their unassailable conviction
that we "were meant to be together," and their insistence that I
yield to her and to the fate that she foresaw for us.

Letters, too, can function like Proust's madeleine, and in the
case of these letters from this woman whom I will call Suzanne
(though she actually had a name given to her by her Yoga guru),
I could not help remembering how it was that we first met and
fell in love. Those letters of hers brought it all back to me, especially the pain we had each suffered because of it. I found myself
drifting back to those fraught days and spent a good hour or more
dwelling on the fever of love which almost destroyed me.

No need to dredge all that up here; those memories will
remain private. In any case, my involvement with her went on
for years. I eventually left the woman I had been living with, but
I could never fully commit myself to Suzanne either. I think now,
as an old man, how my life would have turned out had I chosen
to yield to her. I have both regret and relief that I didn't. My love
for her, however, never ebbed. I can still feel it, especially after
re-reading her letters.

There was one odd thing about her, however, that shows,
I think, how much she felt connected to me. I don't remember

now what her original last name was—it was probably a leftover from her marriage—but one day she told me that she had decided to adopt a new surname. From now on she would be called Suzanne *Ken.*

I laughed; I thought she was joking. But she was serious. And she insisted that her adopting the name Ken had nothing to do with me. But then, why Ken? She wouldn't say other than to aver that it "felt right."

The other night, after re-reading her letters, I couldn't help wondering what had happened to her. I decided to try Googling her, and *mirabile dictu,* I found her. She's 76 now, and living in New England. She is still known as Suzanne Ken.

I have her address. But I will not write to her. What would be the point now? I have to say goodbye to all that, too.

Archives can not only be a bane, and although mine did lead to some rekindling of former friendships, it also made me acutely aware that they can be emotionally dangerous as well. Maybe there are good reasons to leave its contents alone. Maybe that's still another reason for me to get rid of the dang thing.

Anyway, my next step is to try to arrange to do just that. I'm now beginning to look into the possibility that some university or institute would like to take if off my hands and house it.

Preparing to let it go isn't really that difficult. It's just another step in my journey of waiting to die. It will be a big load off my mind to offload all these boxes. Why should they weigh me down when all I want these days is to be able to fly?

CHAPTER SIX

What Hath Roth Wrought?

Philip Roth, who wrote so fiercely about the torments of aging and the calamity of approaching death, has died. In the end it was congestive heart failure that brought his long life to its close. His wait is over.

I can only wonder what his last days were like. I'd like to think they weren't what he had so long imagined them to be, and that he went easy into death with a sense of relief if not of hope. For as he often said, he had none where death was concerned. For him, death simply was extinction. The flickering flame of the candle of life would be snuffed out for good and after that—no after, no nothing, no more Phillip Roth.

In any event, when I heard the news about Roth's death at the age of 85 last week, it was natural for me, as it was for millions of his readers, to think about the man—about his life and work, and perhaps his legacy. What had Roth wrought?

I was never a big fan of Roth's, however. (I was always more partial to his great rival, John Updike.) Of course, I had read a number of his books, beginning with his breakout novella of 1959, *Goodbye Columbus*, when I was just a graduate student hoping to break out in my own way. After Roth's death, I heard an interview with him that had been conducted about ten years earlier in which he told a funny story about that book. He took his parents aside to warn them that the book would almost surely be controversial, and possibly a bestseller, so they should be prepared for attacks on their beloved son. His mother said nothing at the time, but years later Roth learned that afterward she confided to her husband: "Oh, the poor boy. He has delusions of grandeur. He's bound to be disappointed."

And then about a decade later, Roth fulfilled his early promise by writing what is still his best known novel, *Portnoy's Complaint*. And over the many years of his writing career, which didn't end until 2012, he churned out many books, mostly novels, and I read my share, I suppose. Offhand, I can think of his semi-autobiographical *Facts* (of course, many of Roth's books are autobiographical in nature), *The Human Stain, The Plot Against America,* and probably one or more of his Nathan Zuckerman novels—who can remember? I also read a lot *about* Roth who was naturally much written about. Especially damning was the memoir by his second wife, the actress Claire Bloom, who had her trials and grievances with Roth, a difficult and cranky man who prized his solitude. Not a good bet as a husband, and on that, in the end, Bloom lost.

But the book of his that is particularly germane here in these essays about waiting to die is one Roth wrote in 2006, when he was in his early 70s, after he had suffered a number of painful health crises and had begun to ponder what we all do if we live long enough—the horrors of old age and the terrifying specter of death. I use this phrase deliberately, not because I think of aging and death in these ways, but because Roth did.

The book I am referring to is his novella, *Everyman,* which is his meditation on disease, aging, diminishment, pain, loss, loneliness and death. On these subjects, his view is bleak and without hope or consolation. But before we turn to the story that Roth tells in this book in such a chilling way, it will be helpful if we take a brief glance at what Roth himself suffered during the course of his long life.

Actually, since I have not read a biography of Roth, I am not conversant with all of his physical woes, but David Remnick, the editor of The New Yorker, and a good friend, in a brief obituary gave us a quick summary. "He lived to be eighty-five, but he had little expectation of making it much past seventy. Over the years, there had been stretches of depression, surgeries on his back and spine, a quintuple bypass, and sixteen cardiac stents, which must be some kind of American League record." Claire Bloom also recounted some of Roth's other illnesses and surgeries, including occluded arteries and an unsuccessful operation on his knee. After that, he found himself in great pain, suffered from insomnia and nightmares and ultimately had a kind of crack-up, which Bloom ascribed to his use of the drug, Halcion, which was supposed to help him sleep but clearly had the opposite and a psychologically destabilizing effect. Of course, Roth recovered in time. But it's clear that over the span of his life, he was no stranger to serious illnesses and many surgeries.

All this certainly colored the narrative line in *Everyman,* which tells the story, in the third person, of a nameless man (he is "everyman") retrospectively after his death. The book actually opens in a cemetery where he is being buried and toward the end Roth has him visiting his parents' grave in the same cemetery.

The book simply tells the story of this man's life from childhood to the expiration of his life. Talented as an artist, he winds up as an art director in an advertising agency and is quite successful in his career. He marries, has two sons, but finds himself constricted by the routines of marriage and drained by frequent quarrels with his wife, so he leaves them all behind and obtains a divorce. Later, he meets another woman whom he woos and wins, and they marry. After a blissful month's vacation with her, he becomes very ill and is in great pain from what turns out to be a burst appendix, which might have killed him were it not for its discovery at the last moment. But he recovers and lives a healthy life for over twenty years until he has another serious illness. This time it's his heart and it's again life-threatening. He has to endure a seven-hour surgery and undergoes a quintuple bypass operation. By now, he's on his third marriage, after having had a number of affairs, and finding himself alienated from his two boys. His third wife, a former model, is useless and his only close relationship is with his daughter, Nancy, from his second marriage. He will have seven more operations, usually heart-related, before his life comes to an end.

In the book, this man reflects on his life and, as he ages and becomes increasingly preoccupied with his own bodily decay and that of his friends, he finds himself ruing many of the choices he has made in his life. All the pain he has caused his wives, the loss of the affection and respect of his sons, his pointless affairs. Increasingly, wearied by disease, he becomes acutely lonely and clings, almost desperately, to the only person who has remained close to him, his daughter.

Some passages from the book will be helpful to illustrate not just this man's thoughts about the process of aging and the prospect of incipient death, but also Roth's since he, too, is the everyman of whom he writes.

When toward the end of his life, he talks with several of his work colleagues who have become ill with serious diseases like those he has suffered, he thinks:

"Yet what he'd learned was nothing when measured against the inevitable onslaught that is the end of life. Had he been aware of the mortal suffering of every man and woman he happened to have known during all his years of professional life, of each one's painful story of regret and loss and stoicism, of fear and panic and isolation and dread, had he learned of every last thing they had parted with that had once been vitally theirs, and of how, systematically, they were being destroyed, he would have [realized that]....Old age isn't a battle; old age is a massacre."

And he comes to see that he is in exactly the same condition as his colleagues:

Now it appeared that like any number of the elderly, he was in the process of becoming less and less and would have to see his aimless days through to the end as no more than he was—the aimless days and uncertain nights and the impotently putting up with the physical deterioration and terminal sadness and the waiting and waiting for nothing.

The man now finds that his life has become pointless, without meaning, and comments, "All I've been doing is doodling away the time."

Roth has often spoken of his disdain for religion and its empty consolations, which he dismisses as superstitious fantasies unworthy of any intelligent and rational adult, and his character in this book feels the same way:

> Religion was a lie that he had recognized early in life, and he found all religions offensive, considered their superstitious folderol meaningless, childish, couldn't stand the complete unadultness—the baby talk and the righteousness and the sheep, the avid believers. No hocus-pocus about death and God or obsolete fantasies of heaven for him. There was only our bodies, born to live and die on terms decided by the bodies that had lived and died before us. If he could be said to have located a philosophical niche for himself, that was it.

He sums it all up in a tone of savage bitterness as one "who put no stock in an afterlife and knew without doubt that God was a fiction and this was the only life he'd have."

And this is how he goes to his death. This is the death of everyman.

It may surprise you to learn that when I read this book, there was much that I could identify with. I, too, had left wives—I had four—and had to leave two of my children behind after my second marriage collapsed. I have also spent a great deal of time (and wrote one entire confessional book on the subject) reflecting with considerable anguish on my wayward love life and the pain that it had brought to others. And like Roth's character, there have certainly been times in my life recently, during my "waiting to die" period, so to speak, that I have found myself aimless, seemingly just marking time. Particularly when suffering from chronic and painful conditions, I have also become ruefully aware that I was in the midst of mourning the person I used to be who had already died.

Nevertheless, there are many and important differences between me and Roth's character. For one thing, I've been lucky, very lucky, that so far—knock on silicon—I have not had to endure any serious illnesses or undergo any of the kinds of surgeries that Roth or his character did. For another, I have always remained close to my children, even after two them no longer lived with me, and am to this day. But the most important difference of course is my spiritual outlook on life, which was permanently affected by my first psychedelic experience when I was in my mid-thirties and was further deepened by my many years of working with near-death experiencers.

As a result, my view of death is exactly the opposite of Roth's. He is one of those Jewish intellectuals influenced by Freud and the tradition of psychoanalysis that was such a pervasive element in the intellectual lives of East Coast writers and artists who came to maturity during the middle part of the last century. I encountered many of them during my years of working in Connecticut and spending a lot of time in New York. For them, it's the familiar symbol of the grim reaper that represents death, a frightening image indeed. "Life is grim, and then you die." And after that, you disappear for good.

But I, a California Jew, who like Roth has no use for Judaism or any other religion, nevertheless find the teachings of the Buddha far more persuasive than those of Freud concerning how to view illness, decay and mortality. And of course, what has influenced me even more is my many conversations with near-death experiencers who have actually crossed the barrier between life and death, at least for a time, and who almost universally aver with the greatest certitude that there is indeed more to follow once death occurs. For them and for me the real symbol of death in our own time should be "the Being of Light." For Roth death is indeed a dead end. For those who have actually glimpsed beyond the veil, it is just the beginning of true life. For them, when death is encountered, it is not terrifying; instead it has the face of the Beloved.

Roth, an atheist, died in character, and for that we can admire him. But how many of us would really want to live as he did toward the end of his life—often shut up in his cabin chained to his writing desk and striving to hold the enemy, remorseless death, at bay as long as possible? Even after his "retirement" in 2012, he was seemingly unmoored and lost for a time when faced with the end of his career as an author: "I had reached the end. There was nothing more for me to write about. I was fearful I'd have nothing to do. I was terrified, in fact...." He did apparently manage to enjoy himself afterward for a while, but I still wonder, as I remarked at the outset, about the state of his mind when his waiting was finally over and he found himself face to face with death.

I like to think that maybe he was surprised at what he saw.

A necessary postscript: Just because Roth was an almost vehement atheist, I wouldn't want you to suppose that I am implying this is the way that most atheists live and approach death. Far from it. You can be an atheist and go gladly into death or at least without the crippling terror that death had for Roth. Think of David Hume, for example, who seemed to greet death joyfully and with humor. No, there is nothing about atheism *per se* that should make death difficult. But having some kind of spiritual perspective on life does help, and this is precisely what Roth and his everyman lacked. Fortunately, not all of us are that everyman. Roth will leave his legacy for those who are drawn to his view of life—and death. For my part, I choose to leave it, period.

In any case, as I've said, Roth's wait is over. I, on the other hand, am still waiting to die. But I am very far from being eager to approach my terminus. I hope there's still plenty of time before I shout "Can't wait!"

CHAPTER SEVEN

Cheers at the Half

This will be embarrassing, but at least it will be short. The ancient Greeks looked down on anyone who was guilty of false modesty; they felt that if you were a superior person, you should flaunt it. But this ancient Jew feels the opposite, that his modesty is well deserved and any suggestion to the contrary normally makes him cringe. He's the kind of guy who when a compliment is bestowed upon him looks over his shoulder to see who the intended recipient actually is.

All right, you can see where this is leading. Yes, I am going to devote this essay to some good things that have come my way lately, at least in regard to my professional work. My body is another story; it is always something that continues to *need work* as it is continuing to decay at a vertiginous rate. But you have heard me sing that plaint before and don't need to listen to the mournful tune again. Instead, let me turn to some of the things that have made me forget my body for a while and have even cheered me up. They have made waiting to die worth the waiting; for now I'm glad my number hasn't been called just yet.

And, by the way, in case you're wondering about the title of this essay, it refers to the fact that I am writing it on June 13th, 2018, just as I have reached the venerable age of 82 and *a half.*

First, some necessary background. In 1981, two friends and I established the first professional organization to foster research on near-death experiences (NDEs) and to provide support services for those who had had such experiences. I named this organization The International Association for Near-Death Studies (IANDS), established and edited its scholarly journal as well as a newsletter, Vital Signs, and was the first president of IANDS. Of course, I had a great deal of help from other colleagues and my students, which I have always and often acknowledged.

But after a few years, and a second term as president, I turned the running of IANDS over to others so that I could turn back to my real love, researching and writing about NDEs. From that point, I no longer had any formal connection to IANDS.

In the last year, however, the leadership of IANDS sought me out for my putative counsel and invited me to become more involved with its programs. I was flattered but not really tempted, so I declined. But I did agree to write an article or two for its now very glossy newsletter, Vital Signs.

That was my mistake.

For when that issue came out, I was all over it. Not only did it feature my articles, but also some other things about me, an interview, several photographs, etc., all heralded by a huge headline:

2018 UPDATE from IANDS CO-FOUNDER, KENNETH RING, PH.D.

I was being memorialized!

Honestly, though I was touched by all this attention, I was more embarrassed by it, as I wrote to the editor. I really don't like to have the spotlight shined on me, not these days, when I prefer to live quietly in the lame lane of life.

But as things turned out, I guess I'm glad I hadn't been altogether forgotten. Some examples follow, and, as you will see, they seem to form a pattern with meaning.

For one thing, I learned I had a sort of fan club made up of a bunch of people who had been reading and studying of one of my NDE books, *Lessons from the Light.* The leader of the group sent me this photo:

And about the same time, an artist I knew many years ago but hadn't had contact with for eighteen years sent me a package out the blue, a phrase I use deliberately for reasons you will soon understand. In it, this is what I found:

Yep, that was me when I was in my mid-fifties and in my

prime. Sort of. Anyway, no one had ever painted my portrait. It will live on after me, if only maybe in my daughter's attic.

But then I started to receive very warm and appreciative notes from people who had read that issue of Vital Signs. One woman wrote me this:

"My Vital Signs came today. I just read your articles in Vital Signs and I posted (below) on my facebook page because it was a great article. I laughed out loud and every paragraph made me smile. Thank you so much.

In facebook: I'm not feeling at my best and today when my Vital Signs came I lay down to read it. It is absolutely the best one I've read: Ken Ring is hilarious and so true-to-life - and I laughed and laughed. His energy, his tone, his light-touch are perfect."

Another old friend wrote:

I loved the piece you wrote for the recent IANDS newsletter! Sheer joy! As one who is also experiencing the breakdown of the physical body, I could relate to how your story seemed similar to mine, although different. I had to laugh hard.

And then in a subsequent note, she added this, " I am so deeply thankful that you have been such a beautiful part of my life for so many years…. What a party we will have when we reunite again in the afterlife! I'm looking forward to it, but until then, I need to tell you how much I love you and how grateful I am to you for being such a wonderful friend to me."

Naturally, I was very touched by her words, but perhaps the most fulsome (in a good sense) message I received as actually an article entitled, *Remembering Ken Ring.*

What, had I already died? Why didn't somebody tell me?

The article began, "The last issue of *Vital Signs*, dedicated to Ken Ring, caught me. I almost cried, loving every page, every morsel of word and sentence, pictures, memories. Oh, my God, how do I express myself here, my story mixed with his."

She followed up that article with a couple of longer, more

personal letters, full of expressions of love and appreciation, which I won't quote here. But you get the idea. I was getting a lot of love from people who had known me when I was active in my NDE work.

All this made me feel as if I were reading a eulogy before my death.

I began to reflect on what all this attention meant, and eventually I wrote one of these friends the following letter:

I am getting ready to leave. Closing up shop. Heading for the exit. Saying my farewells.

Don't get me wrong. I'm not dying. But I'm getting set for the finale.

Since you read that issue of Vital Signs about me, you already know that I've been writing some essays in a series called "Waiting to Die." I've actually written six of them so far, and some of them have already been published or posted on various websites. They're mostly humorous pieces, written in a light whimsical manner, but always contain something, usually toward the end, with a spiritual message. It's been fun writing them. If I manage to live long enough to write a dozen or so, I might put them into a little book I'm thinking of calling Waiting to Die: Essays on the Road toward Death.

Of course, waiting to die is not the same as preparing to die. The first is passive, the second, active. And both are different from wanting to die, which is conative. I definitely don't want to die (at least not yet, Lord), but I am certainly preparing to. For example, I have started to give away my professional books (I have already got rid of hundreds), made arrangements, when the time comes, to donate all my NDE books and those on death and dying (more hundreds) to IANDS, and have recently been made a wonderful offer from The University of West Georgia to house my entire archive of close to sixty boxes. Over the next two months, I will have to get all those boxes ready to be shipped off to their final resting place, so to speak, before I go to mine.

So much, so far, for my preparations to leave, but what has been happening as I've been doing so is something else entirely, which has been taking place without, I believe, most people knowing what I've been up to lately, namely, getting ready for the last roundup. People have, to my mind, been saying goodbye to me. And in their doing so, I have the distinct impression that it is as if I am a spiritual soldier, and they are saying, as it were, "Thank you for your service." I feel as if I am "being honored" for my work before I die.

For example, take that issue of Vital Signs that you read. Of course, I was pleased to be invited to write some of those little articles for IANDS' members and to be interviewed for that issue. But what has been particularly meaningful to me are some of the very warm responses that that issue has generated, and none more treasured than the one you wrote to me. Now you know why.

Along the same lines and around the same time as that issue of Vital Signs came out has been my contact with a very distinguished European professor and scholar. I had written a short note to him about his research on a phenomenon I was deeply interested in. It's called *terminal lucidity* and refers to a period of complete and clear consciousness that sometimes occurs in severely demented people, such as those suffering from Alzheimer's, shortly before they die. This astonishing phenomenon has interested me keenly ever since I first heard about it years ago from another NDE researcher. In fact, were I still active in research, that's what I would study. Anyway, I wrote to this man, and he responded immediately and warmly. He had read some of my NDE books, and almost made me blush with his words concerning how important they had been to him. A very cordial correspondence has ensued and during the first week, he wrote me six long letters. We were having a kind of bromance, it seems.

In his very first letter, he said he wanted to see a book devoted to honoring us "NDE pioneers" who had formed IANDS, and in each of his subsequent letters he kept returning to that point. He's had some contact with IANDS already, and its president thinks it's a fine idea, so it may happen. At least this wonderful fellow seems bent on seeing this through. But whether it happens or not, his letters and warm friendship have already meant a lot to me.

So perhaps you can see why I think all this forms some sort of a pattern—that I am being given a very nice sendoff by some of those who know and appreciate my work, and who want to convey that to me before I die.

Still, I don't want you to think I am putting on airs, even though my hat size does seem to have increased lately. Nevertheless, I continue to suspect that the good Lord must have confused me with somebody else. If so, I don't wanna know, and if I'm dreaming, please don't wake me up. It's still half time, and though the cheers are beginning to fade, they remain like sweet music to my ears. Waiting to die can have its unexpected pleasures—as long as one isn't in too much of a hurry to get around to it.

CHAPTER EIGHT

Better Dying Through Chemistry

A high dose psychedelic experience is death practice.
—KATHERINE MCLEAN, PSYCHEDELIC THERAPIST

Lately, I've been reading a new book by the celebrated food guru, Michael Pollan, the author of *The Omnivore's Dilemma* and other well known books about food and the food industry. But his new book isn't about food. It's all about psychedelic drugs, and its subtitle tells you exactly what Pollan is on to in this surprising turn in his professional career: *What the New Science of Psychedelics Teaches Us About Consciousness, Dying, Addiction, Depression, and Transcendence.* Wow, about the only thing he left out is the proverbial kitchen sink.

Well, did you *know* that there is such a thing as a "new science of psychedelics?" Indeed there is, and if you haven't noticed, it's actually been going on for the last two decades. And these days it's legit, too, with research programs being carried out by distinguished scholars and academics at some of the leading universities in the U.S. as well as in Europe. Pollan's bestselling book, entitled *How to Change Your Mind,* is an excellent journalistic account of all this work and what we can all learn from it, regardless of whether we have used psychedelics or not.

For me personally, however, it is also a remembrance of trips past because psychedelics were once a pivotal part of my life, and before picking up Pollan's book I was already personally familiar with many of the figures who played an important part in this movement in the days before its recent and surprising re-emergence as an exciting and thriving area of research into the mysteries of consciousness. Yes, Virginia, I, too, had my adventures as a psychonaut back in the day, and this book revived many of those memories....

In these essays, I usually try to stay pretty much in the present tense, and before concluding it I will return there, but to set the stage for what I really want to end up discussing—which *is* our end—I hope you will indulge me for a few moments so that I can describe my own improbable and unplanned entry into a world I had no clue even existed. What I am about to relate was, in fact, the most important thing that ever happened to me, and after it my life was never the same.

In March of 1971, when my then wife and I went off to the Berkshires to celebrate our anniversary, I happened to pick up a book that she was then reading—Carlos Castañeda's first book, *The Teachings of Don Juan*. It looked intriguing and after she had finished it, I read it.

I was then a typical Jewish professor—wedded to rational thought, committed to science and atheistic in my worldview. I had no interest in religion and very little knowledge of mysticism. But I was open to new experiences, and what had particularly excited me about Casteñeda's book was his discussion of what he called "seeing the crack between the worlds," which he had apparently effected through the use of mescaline.

At the time, I had never considered using psychedelic drugs and my only familiarity with anything close was having smoked marijuana a few times. But since I had never been a smoker, even that was difficult for me, and my experiences with it, though of the usual kind, did not have any particular impact on my life.

Nevertheless, since there was a long-haired hippie-ish colleague in my department at the time who I knew was familiar with psychedelics, I approached him to tell him about my interest to take mescaline and why. This fellow was one of those half-crazy/half genius types that most of my colleagues had no use for but whose brilliance and charisma were enough of a compensation to keep him on the faculty. In any case, he had read Castañeda's book and knew what I was after.

I came to the point. Could he provide me with some mescaline? He could.

By then it was early May. The semester was just about over. He told me not to read anything further on the subject and just come to his apartment on the following Saturday.

That day turned out to be a rare beautiful sun-splashed day with everything beginning to bloom. My colleague lived at the edge of a forest. He suggested that I take the mescaline in his apartment, wait just a bit and listen to music and then go outside into the nearby woods.

And then he gave me two purple pills to ingest.

I did not know my colleague well, and as I was soon to find out, he was not only impish, but embodied the trickster archetype. While he gave me to believe I was taking mescaline, he had actually given me 300 micrograms of LSD, a very high dose.

I will not bore you with an account of the next twelve hours. Suffice it to say that all the pillars of my previous ontological categories soon began to crumble into dust. At the time and afterward I realized that this was the most important and most transformative experience of my life—and nearly fifty years later, I still feel the same way. I had the undeniable feeling that I was seeing the world as it really was with pristine eyes. And once I did, I could never return to the person I had been for he, too, had been obliterated.

The one portion of the experience I will allude to here — because it eventually led me to the study of near-death experiences—took place when I was sitting on a log near a stream in the woods. I don't know how long I was there, but at some point for a moment outside of time I—except there was no "I" any longer– experienced an inrushing of the most intense and overwhelming rapturous LOVE and knew instantly that this was the real world, that the universe, if I can put this way, was stitched in the fabric of this love, and that I was home. However, again I have to repeat: There was *only* this energy of love and "I" was an indissoluble part of it, not separate from it.

In fact, I was soon to learn that this experience of "non-duality" in which one becomes aware of the primacy of love is fairly common in psychedelic journeys, and Pollan himself had a similar experience the first time *he* took LSD and comments, as all psychedelic voyagers will attest, at the paucity and seeming banality of using everyday words to describe the ineffable:

> Platitudes that wouldn't seem out of place on a Hallmark card glow with the force of revealed truth.
> *Love is everything.*
> Okay, but what else did you learn?
> No—you must not have heard me; it's *every*thing.

Pollan also mentions that Aldous Huxley had the same insight the first time *he* was given LSD:

> What came through…was the realization…of Love as the primary and fundamental cosmic fact….The words, of course, have a kind of indecency and must necessarily ring false, seem like twaddle. But the fact remains.

And again, in interviewing another psychedelic sojourner, who will allude to where we are going with this, Pollan hears her say: "I remember thinking, if this is death, I'm fine with it. It was…bliss. I had the feeling, no, the knowledge—that every single thing there is is made of love."

This indeed is the exact same revelation that comes to people who have actually experienced the first stages of physical death when they undergo an NDE. Let the following example, which I draw from my book, *Lessons from the Light,* stand for the many accounts of NDEs I have heard over my more than thirty years researching such experiences. This woman was writing of her encounter with a being of light:

> …the light told me that everything was Love, and I mean everything….I vividly recall the part where the light did what felt like switch on a current of pure, undiluted,

concentrated unconditional LOVE. This love I experienced in the light was so powerful it can't be compared to earthly love....It's like knowing that the very best love you feel on earth is diluted to about one part per million of the real thing.

Which brings up a question: If psychedelics can afford direct knowledge of the primacy of love in such an overwhelming way, and if near-death experiencers encounter the same truth when they come close to death, then might it be possible to use psychedelics with terminally ill people to afford them a preview of what they may actually encounter when they die?

> *He who dies before he dies*
> *Does not die when he dies.*
> —ANGELUS SILISEUS 1624-1677

Ketamine is a dissociative anesthetic, which when used at sub-anesthetic levels induces a very distinctive but powerful alteration in consciousness that some people feel mimics the experience of death. In 1984, I was asked by a psychedelic therapist whether I would be willing to participate in a study she was carrying out with an oncologist to determine whether ketamine did induce something like an NDE. (Presumably, I was being tapped for this study because I was an "expert" in such matters—despite never having had an NDE myself.) The idea was that since NDEs almost always cause a loss of the fear of death, ketamine might serve a similar purpose for those *facing* imminent death, such as terminally ill cancer patients.

I eventually did accept the offer and wound up taking it a number of times. I have written about my ketamine experiences elsewhere (those interested will find my account in a book called *The Ketamine Papers,* edited by Phil Wolfson and Glenn Hartelius), and although I personally did not find that they resembled very closely NDEs, others have reported striking similarities. And, indeed, since my own adventures with ketamine, there have been some very promising preliminary case studies reported in which ketamine has significantly reduced fear of death in cancer patients.

Furthermore, beginning in 1965 and continuing into the next decade, the psychiatrist and leading psychedelic therapist, Stanislav Grof, and his colleagues at Spring Grove Hospital in Baltimore, using LSD with terminally ill patients reported the same thing and many other benefits in a significant number of cases.

Finally, Michael Pollan brings us up to date in his book with the latest studies of this kind using psilocybin. Preliminary but very impressive studies have been conducted at both NYU and Johns Hopkins, and once again, 80% of terminally ill cancer patients "showed clinically significant reductions in standard measures of anxiety and depression, an effect that endured for at least six months after their psilocybin session." Moreover, the patients with the best outcomes were precisely those who themselves had had the most complete mystical experiences, presumably akin to an NDE.

These findings astounded even the researchers carrying out these studies. One of then confessed, "I thought the first ten or twenty people were plants—that they must be faking it. They were saying things like 'I understand love is the most powerful force on the planet'....People who had been palpably scared of death—they lost their fear. The fact that a drug given once could have such an effect for so long is an unprecedented finding. We have never seen anything like that in the psychiatric field."

But lest this essay become too academic, let me simply quote a couple of brief excerpts from these patients. First, from a man named Patrick who had these insights during his psilocybin session: *From here on, love was the only consideration...It was and is the only purpose. Love seemed to emanate from a single point of light....I could feel my physical body trying to vibrate in unity with the cosmos.* Aloud he said, "Never had an orgasm of the soul before." And then later, "It was right there in front of me...love...the only thing that mattered."

Next, from Dinah, who described herself to Pollan as a "solid atheist." Nevertheless, Pollan relates that in her psilocybin-induced epiphany, she experienced feelings of "overwhelming love," and later said that she felt herself "bathed in God's love." When Pollan pointed out that using such a phrase would seem to be in contradiction to her professed atheism, she retorted, "What other way is there to express it?"

So from all this, we have learned that psychedelics can be very effective for the terminally ill in helping them overcome the fear of death and their depression about dying, thus enabling them to die with greater serenity and peace of mind. But what about a more radical possibility?

How about administering LSD, *at the very point of death*, so that one goes out riding high on the wave of a psychedelically-induced ecstasy?

Actually, it's been done, and no less by than Aldous Huxley himself whose second wife, Laura, administered LSD to him on his deathbed while urging him to "go toward the light." She has said that he died with "a very beautiful expression on his face." (By an odd stroke of fate, he was having his drug-aided death experience that same day, November 22, 1963, that John Kennedy was assassinated.)

Which as promised brings us back, at last, to the present moment that finds me still waiting for death and thinking again about psychedelics. I'm wondering whether I should follow Huxley and die with the aid of psychedelic agent when my time comes. If it comes.

Check with me later.

Or just read my obit.

CHAPTER NINE

Living with Lauren

One of the things that makes waiting to die a somewhat bitter-sweet experience is my girlfriend Lauren, though I'm sure she would object to being called "a thing." No, she is both my dream girl and the answer to this old man's unspoken prayers. I don't know how I would have survived these past few years without her loving care and all the many things she has done for me during this time to keep the ship of Ring afloat. So it sometimes makes me melancholy when I think that when I die, I will have to leave her behind since the practice of suttee does not seem to be in her repertoire. I will miss her dearly when the time comes for me to take up residence elsewhere.

Lauren and I met online in March, 2015, just as she was about to leave her home in Piedmont, California in order to join her son, Rob, a flight surgeon in the Navy, in Florida where he was to get his "wings." Lauren is, like me, an e-mail junkie, and in the first month of our correspondence, before we had met, we exchanged no fewer than 200 messages, some quite lengthy. I had obviously met my match and the epistolary girl of my dreams. We fell in love writing to each other, but of course we didn't even know each other — we were only words on a screen. All she knew about me by then was that I had apparently been married a dozen times and had had innumerable affairs. I feared this one would turn out to be an affair to dismember.

Lauren is a therapist and like all therapists she had been seeing one for years. Of course, it's a game all therapists play — a racket, in my jaundiced opinion, but never mind. In any case, I imagined the dialogue that would take place when Lauren finally got back home and had a chance to have her next appointment with her therapist.

I call her E. here, which stands for Eliza, my pet name for her, as I often play the insufferable Henry Higgins when we are together for reasons you will soon come to appreciate....

T. Let's see if I can get this straight, Eliza. Are you telling me that you've fallen in love with an old man—pushing 80—that you've never met and have only corresponded with for the last couple of weeks or so?

E. I know it sounds mad....

T. (interrupting). And that he's a Jewish retired professor who has apparently made a career of studying arrant nonsense like near-death experiences and other such pap?

E. Well, I haven't had a chance to look into any of that yet.

T. You mean you only have his word for all this? You haven't even Googled him?

E. I really haven't had time. I've been so busy.

T. Not so busy that you apparently, according to what you told me over the phone, couldn't be writing to him night and day, dozens of e-mail notes and letters, isn't that true?

E. Well, yes, but....

T. (Interrupting again). And didn't you tell me that this old coot has, according to what he's told you, had innumerable lovers and at least four, maybe five, wives already?

E. He's admitted that. He seems pretty honest....

T. Ha! Eliza, don't be naïve. He sounds like an amatory serial killer to me. What in hell are you thinking? That you'll be number 25?

T. (continuing, as Eliza has fallen mute). And didn't you tell me that this guy is, to put it gently, visually challenged and possibly now suffering from some kind of neurological impairment? Are you so addled and besotted that you have forgotten what you went through all those years with Michael?

E. Well, don't I at least deserve a few years of happiness before I die? This man really loves me. I know it and I trust what he says.

T. You know what they say about love, Eliza—that it's blind. Didn't you admit to me that in a loose and unwise moment—maybe when you had drunk too much—that you had indicated to him that you were well-off financially?

E. Well, yes, but....

T. That you even unwisely, for God knows what reason, told him about the diamond mines in your family?

E. I just blurted it out. I know I probably shouldn't have mentioned it.

T. Good Lord, Eliza. How do you know that this Ken is not like some character out of a Henry James novel and is just after your money? What do you know about his financial circumstances?

E. It's never come up. Besides....

T. (Interrupting again). Have you even talked to anyone who knows this man? Anyone who can vouch for him? What about those ex-wives of his? I bet they could give you an earful.

E. (crying). Please—you just don't know him. If you could read what he writes to me.

T. Really, Eliza, anyone can write anything. And a seductive guy like him could easily tell you exactly what you want to hear. For Chrissake, you haven't even met the guy—not that that would answer most of these questions—and you're already almost ready to shack up with him?

E. Don't put it that way. It's so vulgar.

T. I think I've said enough for now. Please think about what I've said and please don't do anything rash. If you decide to explore this, despite all the warning signs and cautions I've mentioned, don't make any decisions without first consulting me, all right? Do you agree?

E. (Reluctantly) All right.

T. I'll see you next time. Better make it in a week before you run off to Mexico with your inamorato.

Well, Lauren never ran off with me to Mexico, but she did take up with me after all despite her reasonable doubts about my amatory history and character. And I can say honestly and truly, I have never been happier with any relationship I have ever had. Lauren is a blessing to me in every way, and guess what, she is not only a superlative cook, a veritable Eloise around the house, but she is literate, charming, fun to be with (in bed and outside of it), and eminently educable about which I will have quite a bit to say in a few moments. And you know what else? She loves to laugh. She writes very amusing e-mail, too. She is a master of drollery and *la aperçu juste*. Occasionally, she even appreciates my sense of humor, though I do sometimes have the feeling she is laughing at me and just humoring me about my quirky sense of humor.

Of course, Lauren is not without a few flaws that blemish her otherwise sterling character. For one thing, she is an ignoramus about film. Apparently Bambi was the last film she had ever seen, so I have spent the last several years conducting a remedial film course for her during which I have introduced her to all the classic American and Foreign films she somehow missed during the course of her adulthood, including virtually every film that Woody Allen ever made. Still, the depth of her ignorance can sometimes be astonishing. Case in point: Just last night, we were watching one of Woody's relatively recent films, "Whatever Works," starring Larry David. At the end, Lauren asked me "Who was that actor that played the lead?"

"You mean Larry David?"

"Is that his name?"

You mean, you don't know who Larry David is??! Do the words, Curb Your Enthusiasm" ring any bells?"

Lauren looked blank. I convulsed in laughter, and soon she was having a laughing fit herself. I laughed until it hurt and tears were streaming down my cheeks.

You can see what I'm up against.

Not long ago, knowing how much I enjoy playing cribbage when my daughter Kathryn visits me, Lauren asked me if I could teach her. Alas, Lauren had a very deprived childhood. Not being Jewish, which wasn't her fault, she grew up never playing cards and continued to call spades "shovels" for a while. But worse was yet to come. It turned out that while Lauren is a wordsmith, she apparently can't count. In cribbage, you have to see certain combinations of cards, such as a run of 3,3,4,5. But Lauren never seemed to be able to see these sets as such. It was as if she could only see the individual cards one at a time, but rarely as a gestalt. A single hand that would normally take five minutes would sometimes take seventeen. Lauren is very deliberate.

There's a part of cribbage when each player lays down his or her cards, and the points of each card are added up. The total can't exceed 31. If a player can't play a card under that value, he or she has to say "Go," and the opponent then gets a point. No card is worth more than ten points (all face cards, for example).

One night a sequence started like this:

I played a 7.

Lauren played a 2, making nine points.

I played a 6, making fifteen.

Lauren shouted "Go!"

I cracked up! She almost had to keep me from falling off my chair.

Lauren also has certain delightful eccentricities. For example, when we take our walks, she will invariably spot a worm and make sure it is kept from clods like me who are apt not even to see it and therefore stomp on it unknowingly. She will risk life and limb to break her car savagely to attend to any road kill that hasn't yet expired. Or to lovingly bury any who have. At her home in Piedmont, she maintains a menagerie that includes not only the usual birds and squirrels, but raccoons and even skunks (!) all of which she feeds and cares for. I will spare you the story about what happened when one of her local skunks decided to pay a visit to her kitchen.

Well, we do love people for their eccentricities (as long as they don't drive us mad), and some of her colossal lacunae in her education do fulfill my irresistible proclivity for displaying my perfect imitation of Rex Harrison in "My Fair Lady."

But I'll tell you something else. Five or so years before I met Lauren, when I was unhappy with my last relationship, I made out a list of what I desire in a woman. Here's what I wrote at the time.

What I Want (and Don't) in a Relationship

1. Shared intellectual interests—in music, literature, art, film, politics, history, Palestine, near-death experiences, spirituality, sports, etc.
   1a. Especially going to classical music concerts, opera, the movies, and eating out.
   1b. And is physically active and basically in good health.
2. Appreciation for my writing and need to write.
3. Someone who is fun to be with—light, funny, romantic.
   3a. Someone whose company I delight in and with whom I can have lively and intellectually rewarding conversation.
   3b. And to whom I am sexually attracted.
   3c. And has a good, preferably quirky, sense of humor.
4. Passion.

5. Someone who is monogamous, loyal, trustworthy, fundamentally honest and true-blue.
6. Someone who can drive at night.
7. Someone who can cook.
8. Someone who appreciates how much my friendships, especially my friendships with women, mean to me and who is not jealous of them.
9. Someone who respects my need to be alone at times.
    9a. And who would be OK with my retaining my own place to live.
10. Someone who has her own creative life, her own circle of friends and is basically independent.
11. Someone who can tolerate my eccentric ways and bodily preoccupations.
12. Someone who, if necessary, could be a good caretaker and who, if the situation calls for it, could be nurturant.
13. Someone who likes or at least can get along with my friends and family.
14. Someone who can be happy with mostly intra-California and domestic traveling—which is not to say that some traveling abroad wouldn't be possible, my health permitting.
15. Someone who is basically self-supporting.

And guess what again? Lauren satisfies *every one* of these criteria. That's why I say she's my dream girl. I dreamed her up, and now I have the girl of my dreams.

It's enough to make a man think twice about waiting to die.

If I can't change my mind, well, at least I can dally. With Lauren there is just too much fun to think about death, even though I sometimes think I will die laughing after she makes another risible blunder while playing cribbage. There are, I suppose, worse ways to die.

CHAPTER TEN

Detouronomy

A funny thing happened to me on the road toward death.

I got sidetracked and wound up taking a detour.

These days, it seems, I am being courted, and my life, at least my professional life, appears to be heading in a new and unexpected direction. If this keeps up, it is even possible that I will have to put my death on hold.

The first thing that caused a change in my life in the last couple of months has to do with my archive. You may remember that I have already written about my archival agonies and how I wound up being stuck with more than fifty boxes of my stuff and had no idea what was to become of it, much less what was to become of me.

Well, at least I now know the answer to my first quandary.

In May, I received a most surprising letter from the archivist at the University of West Georgia to whom I had written in what I thought was probably a vain hope that she might be interested in my holdings. I had selected this university because I already knew that it had just the kind of archival resources I was looking for and was open to research dealing with the paranormal.

I had almost given up hearing back from the archivist after several weeks had passed since I had sent my letter of inquiry, but then I received this note, after speaking to the archivist at last:

"It was wonderful to speak to you today. I just read the August 28, 1988 *New York Times* interview. [She was referring to an article about me and my work.] It shows, as I have heard from listening to you, your curiosity about the human experience and your care for humans. I deeply appreciate that. I am also professionally thrilled to have your papers at UWG. They will be a tremendous research collection on near death and other anomalous experiences for years to come. Thank you!"

Yippee!

Lauren and I have spent the last month and more again inspecting the contents of my boxes, both at my home and at her art studio, labeling and then taping up them for pick-up by UPS, which is a whole other story, filled with inexplicable delays, misunderstandings, changed schedules and other hassles, but, finally, just last week, the last trove of boxes was shipped off to Georgia where they will be catalogued over the next few months and eventually be made available to scholars and researchers interested in NDEs.

What a relief to see those boxes on the way to Georgia.

But that is not the only event that has recently occurred in my life involving a university in Georgia. A few weeks ago, I learned that a woman named Lisa, who was apparently connected in some way to Raymond Moody, the man who coined the phrase, "near-death experiences," was attempting to get in touch with me on Raymond's behalf. However, what was peculiar about this overture was the improbable and circuitous route that this woman had followed in an effort to reach me.

She had taken the trouble to track down the Palestinian co-editor of a book I had published some years ago on the lives of contemporary Palestinians! My friend had written me simply to forward Lisa's message to me. He could only wonder why she had had to go by way of Ramallah to find me in California!

Anyway, the message was simple: Raymond Moody does not use computers, but wanted to talk with me. Lisa was asking me to get in touch with her in order to make the connection between Raymond and me.

I sent Lisa a brief e-mail and said, in effect, "What's up with this?" It was then I heard about that other university in Georgia.

But first, a little background is necessary to fill you in on my relationship with Raymond Moody. We first met at the University of Virginia in November, 1977, when a few of us early NDE researchers gathered in order to figure out how best to develop a field of study concerned with NDEs. Raymond, who was then in his early thirties, and who charmed us all with his humor and humility, was still pursuing work toward his M.D. (he had already obtained a Ph.D. in philosophy and been a professor of philosophy), and needed to get back to it. He was eager to "pass the torch," as it were, to us pioneer researchers, and we were just as avid to grasp it and continue to light the way. A few years later, we had our organization, The International Association for Near-Death Studies (IANDS).

In those early years, I saw a lot of Raymond since we attended IANDS meetings together and often were featured speakers at conferences. It was always a delight to spend time with him; Raymond is enormously entertaining with an antic personality and a brilliant mind. But after a few years, we didn't see each other as often as we followed quite divergent paths in our work. And since Raymond doesn't do e-mail and hates to talk on the phone as much as I do, we hadn't had any contact for about the last ten years or so.

But now he wanted to speak with me. Howcum?

As Lisa explained it to me in an a-mail, Raymond wanted to tell me about a new university he was starting up in Georgia. He was calling it "The University of Heaven." Lisa said that the plan was to offer various courses on NDEs and other death-related phenomena, to publish various books on those subjects and to offer regular webinars for those interested in such subjects. Raymond wanted to interview me for one of those webinars, and, moreover, he wanted me to become, as it were, a member of the University of Heaven faculty.

Oh, brother! "The University of Heaven." Give me a break. I immediately objected to Lisa about the name of this dubious enterprise. I started to call it "Woo Woo U," and was sure satirists would have a field day making fun of it.

But Lisa herself was very charming, articulate and persuasive, and in a spate of e-mails that followed in short order, she began making me a series of offers I was finding hard to resist. They would sell my books—not only my NDE books, but some of my other books as well. They would give me my own blog or column in which I could then publish these essays. Because of Raymond's celebrity I could then reach a very large audience. They would even publish my book of these essays once I had written enough of them. They would make me famous again!!

Other blandishments followed. I demurred for a time, but gradually softened and began to think that I might actually allow myself to be wooed.

After a month or so of these e-mails (I never did speak to Raymond), Lisa mentioned that since she had family in the Bay Area, she would be leaving Georgia soon to see them. We could meet. And just yesterday we did—for a riotous and highly enjoyable two hour lunch.

During that lunch, she pretty much won me over. And to seal the deal, she brought me a t-shirt. Here I am, wearing it.

Now at the same time I had been corresponding with Lisa, I had also been receiving a series of friendly letters from a woman named Tricia who had had an NDE in 1992, and who in the last few years had been making a name for herself. I had first heard about Tricia from a good friend of mine interested in NDEs. He had met her and had become a good friend. He told me that she had written a marvelous book about her NDE and that she was already developing quite a following. He then sent me one of her YouTube videos, and I could see for myself why my friend had been so taken with her.

Now Tricia was writing to me, saying she, too, would be visiting California and was hoping to meet and interview me on YouTube. Oh, God, first Raymond, and now Tricia. I hate being interviewed and have steadfastly refused all comers in recent years. Lately, my excuse had been based on a dictum of the late Kenneth Clark, the famous art historian, who in one of his memoirs said that no man (his sexist language, not mine) over seventy should permit himself to appear in public.

Tricia was having none of it.

We left it open, but I agreed to meet her with her and her boyfriend who was in effect her cameraman. Prior to her visit, however, Tricia, too, sent me a number of letters about herself and her NDE work, and also e-mailed me the first three chapters of her book. They were riveting and very well written (I later learned that she had taught courses in creative writing at a community college.) Tricia was also making another conquest of me—the woman could write.

We met just this week also, a couple of days before I had my lunch with Lisa. And the three of us had a really fabulous time together. For me, it was like old times being able to converse with an NDEr about her life and her NDE. However, I was too tired that day to consent to an interview—I will resort to any excuse to beg off—but we wound up doing a sort of interview, anyway, that will be posted on her website, where she also wanted to post some of my essays.

Now, here's where it gets gnarly. In a loose moment some

weeks ago, I had apparently agreed to give Lisa exclusive rights to publish these essays, but I had completely forgotten that promise. Oops! Now, these two women—who turn out to know each other and are friends—were contending for the rights to publish these essays. (Well, to be accurate, Tricia hadn't known about my previous agreement with Lisa, so she wasn't really aware of this.) But in a way, I felt I had to head off a kind of potential "bidding war" before a fractious feud broke out between friends.

So here I am, heading toward 83, and still being coveted by attractive women. Who has time to die? Why even bother? I have been deterred.

Addendum: The office manager of IANDS has called to tell me of an exciting new development. A wealthy Florida woman, a benefactor of IANDS, wants to build an NDE museum and library, and wants me involved.

"But," I protested, "I haven't had any formal involvement with IANDS for over thirty years. I'm just a has-been who wants to be left alone."

"No, Ken," she responded, "you're an *icon!*"

This woman, too, apparently won't take no for an answer. She has threatened to call me next week.

Stay tuned. This may turn out to be a longer detour than I had counted on. If people continue to pester me, my waiting for death may just have to wait.

CHAPTER ELEVEN

Nothing To Be Frightened Of

I should not really object to dying
were it not followed by death.

—D. J. ENRIGHT OR PERHAPS JULIAN BARNES,
OR WAS IT THOMAS NAGEL? POSSIBLY ALL THREE.

Dying is hard; death is easy.

—GUESS WHO

For me, death is the one appalling fact that defines life; unless you are constantly aware of it, you cannot begin to understand what life's about. Only a couple of nights ago, there came again that alarmed and alarming moment, of being pitchforked back into consciousness, awake, alone, utterly alone, beating pillow with fist and shouting, "Oh no Oh no OH NO" in an endless wail, the horror of the moment. I say to myself, "Can't you face down death?" Can't you at least protest against it more interestingly than that? For God's sake, you're a writer; you do *words*. We know that extreme physical pain drives out language; it's dispiriting to learn that mental pain does the same.

No, that's not me talking. You should know that by now.

Any guesses? The title of this essay should give you a hint since it's the title of a book he published about ten years ago.

OK, he's English. Primarily known as a novelist. Winner of the Man Booker Prize and many other literary honors.

Give up?

He's Julian Barnes, and he has a dread of death.

The account above, which I've condensed from the original, is just one example of what Barnes, who is an avid Francophile, likes to call *le réveil mortel*—an awakening with a sudden overwhelming terror of death.

I've been reading Barnes's novels on and off for years, beginning with one of his best known early books, *Flaubert's Parrot*, of which I'm embarrassed to say I now remember nothing except that I was drawn to it by its intriguing title. But in recent years, I've returned to Barnes with pleasure and have read a number of his last spate of books, most of which strike a certain reflective elegiac tone. Among them, *The Sense of an Ending,* which is the book that was awarded the Man Booker Prize; *The Noise of Time,* a book based on some critical incidents in the life of the Russian composer, Dmitri Shostakovich; *Levels of Life,* a book in three parts that ends with a haunting and harrowing memoir of grief following the death of his wife, Pat Kavanagh; and, just now, another novel in three parts, *The Only Story.*

But the book I want to dwell on in this essay, one written just before the death of his wife and published in 2008, the very year of her death, is Barnes's meditation on death with the cunning title, *Nothing To Be Frightened Of.* On the contrary, however. As the book, at times unabashedly confessional but often laced with humor, makes clear, for most of Barnes's life, beginning when he was a young teenager, he has been obsessed with death and has come to dread it. For him, as he has remarked in more than one book, there is no God, no afterlife, only extinction and eternal nothingness. Just the inevitable passage toward this unspeakable abyss fills him with horror.

A friend asks him how often he thinks about death, and Barnes replies:

> At least once each waking day….and then there are the intermittent nocturnal attacks—what Barnes again calls *le réveil mortel* and goes on to elaborate with the help of a metaphor.

How best to translate it? "The wake-up call to mortality" sounds a bit like a hotel service....It is like being in an unfamiliar hotel room, where the alarm clock has been left on the previous occupant's setting, and at some ungodly hour you are suddenly pitched from sleep into darkness, panic and a vicious awareness that this is a rented world.

This is the sudden eruption of the terror of death, a kind of cosmic panic attack from which there is really no escape, only a temporary surcease until it recurs.

Writers seem to be particularly susceptible to such overwhelming frissons at the thought of death. Barnes recounts one such frightening incident in the life of Zola who seems to have been a particularly death-haunted person. Zola was part of a group of writers—all atheists or resolute agnostics—who used to meet at the Magny restaurant in Paris. It was a distinguished group that included, besides Zola, such literary eminences as Flaubert, Turgenev, Edmond de Goncourt and Alphonse Daudet.

In 1880, the year of Flaubert's death, when Zola was forty, *le réveil mortel* seems to have struck him with a shuddering impact. Zola was apparently unable to sleep and was gripped by what Barnes describes as "mortal terror." He later confessed all this to the remaining members of the Magny group, and Goncourt recorded it for his diary. Zola's confession and Flaubert's recent death got them all talking about death and eventually elicited a similar confession from Daudet about his own morbid obsessions about death.

Incidentally, there is an ironic coda concerning the death of Zola twenty years later. Zola was known to have imagined a kind of *belle mort* for himself where he would die in a sudden dramatic accident. He did in fact die in one, but not the kind he had envisioned for himself. He died of carbon monoxide poisoning in his bed.

This in fact is one of Barnes's great themes. He gives many examples of people imagining the way that they will die or would like to die, and then it turns out that their actual deaths are nothing like those suppositions and often take the form of a nasty surprise. As Barnes remarks:

> "We shall probably die in hospital, you and I." A foolish thing to write, however statistically possible. The pace, as well as the place, of our dying is fortunately hidden from us. Expect one thing and you will likely get another.

He then goes on to mention that the death of one of his favorite French authors, Jules Renard. When Renard turns forty-four, he thinks he may not double his years and die at eighty-eight. He was right, but his death came a lot sooner than he had imagined. By the next year, he could hardly walk and was dead at forty-six. Ya never know. Another reason that Barnes is spooked by death.

The poet Philip Larkin was still another writer who was preoccupied with thoughts and fears about death -- and what would come after. In one of his poems, he wrote these lines:

> Not to be here
> Not to be anywhere
> And soon; nothing more terrible, nothing more true

A biographer tells us that in his fifties, "the dread of oblivion darkened everything," and by his sixties, his fears became even more evident. Larkin himself wrote, "I don't think about death all the time, though I don't see why one shouldn't, just as you might expect a man in a condemned cell to think about the drop all the time. Why aren't I screaming?"

Larkin's own death was particularly and perhaps predictably ghastly. A friend visiting him the day before Larkin's death testified, "If Philip hadn't been drugged, he would have been raving. He was that frightened."

Barnes alludes to other famous writers whose psyches, likewise, were tormented by thoughts of death, including Kingsley Amis (whose early book, *Lucky Jim,* had me in stitches when I read it) and the poet, John Betjeman. Even the great Goethe, according to the doctor who attended him when he lay dying, went to his death "in the grip of a terrible fear and agitation."

Not content to frighten us by parading his roster of death-fearing writers before us, Barnes also devotes considerable attention to composers who were obvious "thanatophobes." Rachmaninov is a well known exemplar of this condition, and Barnes aptly characterizes him as "a man both terrified of death, and terrified that he might survive afterward." Shostakovich is another familiar case. Among many other statements he made about death were these remarks: "Fear of death may be the most intense emotion of all. I sometimes think there is no deeper feeling."

As a kind of sidebar to give us a break from these morbid souls, as a lover of classical music myself and as one who has written a couple of books about classical composers, I couldn't help noticing how often Barnes would make references to them; they are strewn throughout his book. I eventually started making a list of them. Besides Rachmaninov and Shostakovich, Barnes alludes to Haydn, Mozart, Brahms, Ravel, Stravinsky, Rossini, Chabrier, Prokofiev and Bruckner—and I might have missed some!

He gives particular attention to Ravel because, I feel sure, what happened to him in his later years is especially tragic and horrifying. Which of course is just the sort of depressing grist that Barnes is keen to grind out to stoke our own fears of death.

As it happens, when I was writing about classical composers, I had read several books about Ravel, so I was already familiar with the story Barnes relates after Ravel began suffering from a form of cerebral atrophy during the last five or so years of his life. Believe me, you would wince in tearful sympathy to read it, so I will spare you the details. But toward the end, Ravel could no longer recognize his own music. At times this became almost comical and not just heartbreaking. After a performance of one of his pieces, the audience rose to salute him. But Ravel thought they were applauding the man next to him, so he joined in the applause. (By the way, the same thing happened to Chabrier, who died of tertiary syphilis. He was also eventually unable to recognize the opera he had written—like Ravel, he thought it was the work of another composer.)

In a kind of macabre way, Barnes seems almost to relish narrating these stories, and there are far worse ones in his book, because he wants his readers to know how much can go wrong in our lives even before death, and why any sane person might well go nearly insane when it comes to thinking about death itself. "Nothing to be frightened of" indeed.

How did Barnes come to have the views he propounds in this book, as if to wake us from what we've been denying—the terrifying specter of death and the undeniable fact that it represents the absolute extinction of one's personality?

Barnes grew up in a non-religious home, and comments, almost with pride, that he was "never baptized, never sent to Sunday school [and that he has] never been to a normal church service in my life." His only sibling, a brother who became a philosopher, was likewise a non-believer and told Barnes that he had never "lost his faith" since he never had any and thought "it was a load of balls."

By the time he reaches Oxford, he tells the college chaplain that he is "a happy atheist," and, one gathers, so are most of his friends.

Once he becomes a well known writer, his views about religion are pretty much set—"No God, no heaven, no afterlife," as he pithily puts it. And the writers he most admires—those from the past as well as the present—seem mainly to hew to a similar perspective, one in which God has no purchase. Barnes, too, comes to have his own Magny-like group, except it meets in Soho, and at the time of his writing his book on death, it is down to seven men, most in their sixties and seventies. When one night the conversation turns to a consideration of belief in an afterlife, "five and three-quarters" give it no credence, the fractional party calls religion a 'cruel hoax,' yet admits he 'wouldn't mind if it were true."

This, then, is Barnes' intellectual milieu. The writers he honors are mostly from the same skeptical tribe and share the same mindset. This is his reference group; these are the people whose esteem he understandably cherishes. In a sense, they are the sorts of people he must have in mind when he writes his books.

So, naturally, he will make fun of and mock those who are religious and still believe, and seems to take delight in the fact that the great churches of England and Western Europe are these days mostly empty or just filled with tourists. After all, in a world after Darwin, Nietzsche and Freud had sent God packing, who can believe in this kind of superstitious crap any longer? It's unseemly.

And an afterlife? Barnes pokes fun at that too, as if to say, were he an American, "Give me a *break!*" At one point in this connection, he refers to Arthur Koestler, who:

> ...before committing suicide, left a note in which he expressed "some timid hopes for a depersonalized afterlife."

> Such a view is unsurprising—Koestler had devoted many of his past years to parapsychology—but to me is distinctly unalluring. Just as there seems to be little point in a religion which is merely a weekly social event... so I would want my afterlife, if one's on offer, to be an improvement—preferably a substantial one—on its terrestrial predecessor. I can just imagine slopping around half-unawares in some gooey molecular mix, but I can't see that this has any advantage over complete extinction. Why have hopes, even timid ones, for such a state?

Barnes continues for another paragraph or two with more droll sarcasm of this kind, and he does seem to turn the idea of an afterlife into a complete absurdity. But here I have to interrupt where I want to take this essay for a moment to say that I am really being a bit unfair to Barnes. There is so much more in his book than I have indicated—a lot about his family, for example—that is witty, engaging, and wonderfully entertaining.

He is a marvelous storyteller, as you would expect from a great novelist, which he is, and his book is full of memorable and amusing anecdotes (if you read it, be sure to look for the one about Rossini as an old lecher). But still....

But still, Barnes is woefully and perhaps willfully ignorant, it seems, about what has been happening for more than the last forty years in a world away from the one in which he has been immersed. I'm referring, of course, to all the research that has been done during that time on the near-death experience and similar phenomena. That research has given us an entirely new understanding of death (actually, it is a very old one; it's just been out of fashion for a long time) and is just one line of evidence, of several, that has made the case for survival of bodily death not only plausible, but almost impossible to deny. I submit that any person who is curious enough to examine this literature with an open mind will come to see that the accumulated body of evidence that has been amassed during this period clearly points to the conclusion that life is not a dead end and does not, as Barnes avers, end either in extinction or cosmic goo.

Ah, Julian, why don't you read my books since I have now read so many of yours? Something has happened since your Oxford days, and you haven't been paying attention. You might just have to reconsider some of your views!

Actually, Barnes might have already missed his chance when he was a young man. At that time, he was a journalist and one day came to interview an elderly novelist...

then in his eighties, frail and bed-bound; death was not far away. At one point he picked up from his bedside table an anthology about immortality, and showed me a heavily underlined account of an out-of-body experience. This, he explained, was identical to one he had himself undergone as a soldier in the First World War. "I believe in resurrection," he said simply. I was awkwardly silent. "No, well, nor did I at your age," he went on sympathetically. "But I do now."

Barnes adds: "So perhaps I shall change my mind (though I doubt it)." Ken adds,"It's not too late, Julian!"

Well, of course, Barnes will never read these words and it's also doubtful that at his age—he is now 72—he will start perusing the literature on NDEs, yet if he did, he would not only find evidence pointing to survival, but to the fact that as you enter through the portal of death, you take your personality with you, as NDErs attest. Let one example stand for many. One woman I interviewed told me that during her NDE, she found herself standing in a mist, "and I knew immediately that I had died and I was so happy that I had died, but I was still alive. And I cannot tell you how I felt. It was, 'Oh, God, I'm dead, but I'm here. I'm me!'" As the title of one recent book, which provides abundant documented evidence for the authenticity of NDEs, puts it, *The* Self *Does Not Die.*

And it's not just the research on NDEs that is giving us a new view of death. There's other research that is helping us to understand dementia in a new way, too. Barnes in his book relates some very distressing instances of people in demented states, and both of his parents eventually suffered debilitating strokes as well. Of course, these are the things we all dread and what makes the end of life for so many a fearful calamity, and yet it is not the whole picture. Consider, for example, the work on what is called "terminal lucidity."

It refers to a situation like this. Let's say you have an aged relative—let's make him your grandfather—who has had Alzheimer's for years during which time he has never been able to speak. Whoever he was seems to have disappeared leaving only the shell of his body. But then, astonishingly, shortly before his death, his eyes brighten, he is able to talk as lucidly as ever, and is able say how much he has always loved you, etc. He's clearly back in his full and familiar personality.

You are amazed and thrilled—but then, he becomes unconscious and not long afterward dies.

What to make of this? Was he there all along and just not able to break through until the end? How is such a thing possible when his brain has suffered irreversible damage?

You'd be surprised how often this sort of thing occurs, even though until recently there hasn't been much research on it. But I've been in touch with some of the leading researchers of terminal lucidity in this country and abroad and have a keen interest in their work. Heck, if I weren't pushing 83 and hampered by the trials of creeping decrepitude, that's what I'd be researching now!

One more piece of evidence that something entirely unexpected—and profoundly comforting and reassuring—can occur at the point of death. I am reminded of a line in Auden's long poem, "For the Time Being," that goes,"We who must die demand a miracle." Maybe terminal lucidity qualifies.

But returning to NDEs, I have saved the best news for last for people like Barnes who find themselves terrified by the thought of death. And here it is in a nutshell: *The greatest antidote to the fear of death, and what will quash it, is having an NDE!* Of course, not everyone can have an NDE, but as I point out in my book, *Lessons from the Light,* anyone who takes the trouble to look into and absorb the insights from NDEs can begin to reap for themselves many of their benefits, including the loss or sharp diminishment of the fear of death.

In any case, when I was first researching NDEs forty years ago, I collected testimonies from NDErs about the effects of their experience on their fear of death. Here's a small sampling of what they told me:

> I had been terrified of death before, it [the NDE] left me with a total lack of fear of death.
> Well, I certainly have no fear of death.
> I'm not afraid of death at all.
> I have no fear of death. I don't to this day.
> If this is what death is like, then I'm not afraid to go....I have absolutely no fear at all.
> I have no fear of death.
> I'm not afraid of dying. I'm really not afraid and I used to be scared to death.

I collected many such quotes from this research (but there is no point in endlessly listing them here) and all other NDE researchers have reported the same findings.

It's probably too late for Barnes to learn and take heart from these experiences, but presumably not for you, if you still find yourself fearful of death. Read the literature on NDEs, or better yet, talk to NDErs. It's one of the best ways I know to conquer the fear of death.

But all this, to be sure, doesn't fully address all aspects of Barnes's fear. Quite apart from the fear of death, what about the *fear of dying?*

Of course, NDEs don't do anything to diminish that. It's understandable to fear dying. If old age isn't for sissies, dying is surely not for the craven. Let's not kid ourselves; no one looks forward to dying (except those in extreme pain or those who are simply weary of life). And who knows what dying will be like for us? Who can say whether when the time comes, we will die "in character?" Elisabeth Kübler-Ross, the great expert on death, apparently had a very difficult time dying and was very angry. Who knows whether Ken Ring, the guy who spent half his life studying NDEs, won't die like Tolstoy's Ivan Illich by screaming for three days before his death? It's a crapshoot and you don't have the chance to load the dice.

Still, there's another way to look at this, and one that puts it in a more hopeful frame. Women know the pain of childbirth, but every person is eventually going to have to go into labor in order to jettison the body, to give it back. Women rightly fear childbirth; we all are right to fear dying. But afterward women have their babies and rejoice, and all of us who have to endure the possible agony of dying will be granted *a second birth* into a new life, which promises wonders of its own. Who would not look forward to that?

To end, perhaps you'll permit me a personal word, one that will allow me to come back full circle to the beginning of this essay and Barnes's *le réveil mortel.*

When I was a boy I rarely thought about death. Perhaps that

was because no one close to me had died. Perhaps it was because I was not very imaginative. But I was not the kind of kid who would wake up during the night, terrified by the thought that one day I would die. So I never had my own *réveil mortel*. I was too busy thinking about baseball and girls to concern myself with the prospect of my death in the far distant future.

But now that I am well past eighty and waiting to die, I naturally think about death quite a lot. However, because I have been privileged to have talked to many hundreds, perhaps more than a thousand, near-death experiencers since 1977 during a long career as an NDE researcher and author, I no longer have any fear about death itself. Like virtually all NDErs who have lost their fear of death, mine has dissolved mainly because, I think, of my long immersion in near-death studies.

Instead of fear, I am ever more *curious* about what I will find when I die, assuming I ever get around to it. I have heard so many stories of what death is like. And I remember what Melville wrote about death's affording a last revelation that only "an author from the dead" could adequately tell. But what will *I* experience, if anything at all? That remains a mystery, a complete unknown. All my research concerning the experience of dying avails me no certainties about my own death. Life is an adventure, but the greatest adventure yet to come still lies ahead shrouded in darkness. But we know what follows darkness, don't we?

CHAPTER TWELVE

The Body is a Sometimes Thing

The blind receive sight and the lame walk,
the lepers are cleansed and the deaf hear,
and the dead are raised up.
—MATTHEW II:5

Death is no more than passing from one room into
another. But there's a difference for me, you know.
Because in that other room I shall be able to see.
—HELEN KELLER

A middle-aged man, with a paunch, is sitting on a doctor's examining table waiting anxiously for the doctor to return with the results of his latest examination.

The doctor comes in, looking solemn.

"I'm afraid it's your body," he intones.

I am that man. Surely Yeats did not have me or my body in mind when he wrote his immortal lines, "things fall apart, the center cannot hold," but they are apposite, I'm afraid. Somatic entropy is icumen in.

I don't want to bore you with a list of my various infirmities and debilities since I already regaled you with those woes in the very first essay in this series, which I wrote in December, 2017. I'm tempted just to write something along the lines of, "suffice it to say, they have all grown worse." But I will resist that temptation if you will indulge me for a few moments in order to give you some specifics. Besides, as usual, I have an ulterior motive for mentioning some of them, which will shortly be revealed.

To begin with, I now list. That is, these days when standing or walking, I am no longer an orthogonal being. Instead, following my political proclivities, I tilt to the left. Generally, I am not aware of this until I run into a lamppost or something, which is a painful way of being reminded that I now am an embodiment of the same principle as the Leaning Tower of Pisa. (You can see photographic evidence of this if you scroll back to the tenth essay in this series where there is photo of me, tilting, while wearing a University of Heaven t-shirt.)

And then there is my difficulty in walking, quite apart from my wayward posture. For one thing, I have now acquired not just a paunch of my own, but a pot. I joke that having once written a book entitled *Heading Toward Omega,* I could now write another called *Heading Toward Rotundity.* Hell, I am only heading toward death, but I have already achieved full rotundity. And this in a man who was once described as a "slender mustachioed researcher." The pounds don't come off easily any longer; they adhere, having found a cozy home of their own in my belly and seek to expand like a balloon filling with air, even when I *think* about consuming another York Mint Patty. The result is, I no longer just walk; it's more that I now waddle, and sometimes wobble, in the general direction of my destination, drawing piteous and condescending stares, and sometimes curses, from the buff young Marinites who have to swerve to avoid hitting me with their bikes on the walking path that runs along the creek adjacent to my home.

But that's only the beginning of my current travails. Worse still is what causes me to mutter, "ai, ai, eye!" Yes, it's my eye, or rather it's the lack of vision in one of them. (And, BTW, I can't resist mentioning to you that for years I saw an eye doctor named—Dr. Ai. No, I am not kidding. He was a retinal specialist, and that was really his name. I managed to refrain making the obvious joke whenever I saw him.) But back to my eye.

I have had glaucoma for over twenty years, and recently it's got quite a bit worse. When you have glaucoma you are regularly tested to see how much peripheral vision you have lost. Would you like to see the latest results for my right eye?

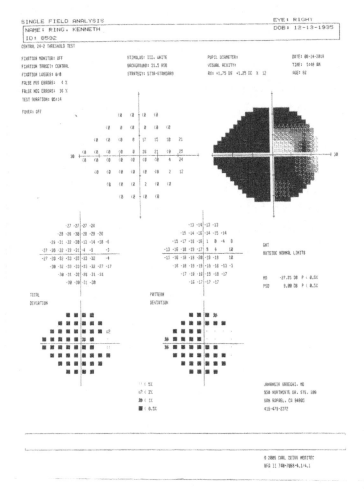

Ignore all the numbers. Just look at the picture with all the black shading. Wherever you see black, that's what I *don't* see. So, you can see that I am completely blind on the left side of that eye, and have only a little sliver of vision in my right visual field. In addition, I have what's called a macular pucker (or wrinkle) in that eye that interferes with my central vision. When I try to look at the Snellen chart (the chart that eye doctors use to check your vision), the best I can do is 20/200.

So to put all this into technical terms, that eye is shot. In order to see anything, I have to depend on my left eye, which isn't nearly so compromised by glaucoma, but it ain't so great either.

Are you beginning to get an idea of my visual world? Unfortunately, my vision has deteriorated quite a bit since I started writing these essays. Nowadays, I don't see as much as I *infer* the existence of what we were once pleased to call the external world. I mean, if the street where I walk was there yesterday, I assume it must still be there today. But my vision is getting to be a joke. For example, the other day, as I was completing my warm-down after my stint on my stationary bike, I happened to pass by my next door neighbor, who was walking her dog. I did recognize that a dog was coming toward me, but I failed to recognize my neighbor. Just call me Mr. Magoo of Marin.

Well, you can see—no pun intended since that verb is largely conjectural for me now—that I have my reasons for hoping that I won't have to wait too much longer to have better vision. No, there is no operation that can help me.

The only thing that can—is death! And now I will tell you why I have cause to think that one day, perhaps before too long, I will have *perfect* vision.

One of things that first struck me so forcibly when I was starting out on my life as an NDE researcher was how often my respondents would comment on how well they could see (and hear) during their NDEs. Here are some of those remarks from my first book on NDEs, *Life at Death.*

I could see very clearly, yeh, yeh. I recognized it [her body] as being me.
My ears were very sensitive at that point...Vision also.
I heard everything clearly and distinctly.
Seems like everything was clear. My hearing was clear...I felt like I could hear a pin drop. My sight—everything was clear.

It was as if my whole body had eyes and ears.

Years later, one of my students, who had had an NDE, and who had previously lost most of the hearing in one of his ears, told me he could hear *perfectly* during his NDE.

And it's a similar story for people who are poorly sighted, but not during their NDE. Consider the following case of a 48-year-old woman who reported this experience following post-surgical complications. All of a sudden:

> Bang. I left. The next thing I was aware of was floating on the ceiling. And seeing down there, with his hat on his head [she is referring to her anesthesiologist]…it was so vivid. I'm very near-sighted, too, by the way, which was another one of the startling things that happened when I left my body. I see at fifteen feet what most people see at 400…They were hooking me up to a machine behind my head. And my first thought was, "Jesus, I can see! I can't believe it, I can see!" I could read the numbers on the machine behind my head and I was just so thrilled. And I thought, "They gave me back my glasses."

> Things were enormously clear and bright…From where I was looking, I could look down on this enormous fluorescent light…and it was so dirty on top of the light. [Could you see the top of the light fixture, then? I asked.] I was floating above the light fixture. [Could you see the top of the light fixture?] Yes [sounding a little impatient with my question], and it was filthy. And I remember thinking, "Got to tell the nurses about that."

Even more astonishing than the fact that those with defective vision seem to see perfectly during their NDE is the finding from my own research on the blind (he said modestly) that clearly shows that even persons who are congenitally blind—people who obviously have never seen in their lives—*can* and do see during their NDEs. As one of these persons who I interviewed for my book, *Mindsight,* where I present about thirty of these cases, and who had had two NDEs, said: "Those experiences were the only time I could ever relate to seeing, and to what light was, because I experienced it. I was able to see."

This testimony comes from a woman named Vicki who was 43 when I first met and interviewed her in Seattle. In the course of her interview she told me that during her (second) NDE, when she was 22, which took place in a hospital, she found herself up by the ceiling and could clearly see her body below (she recognized it from seeing her hair and also her wedding ring). She continued to ascend and eventually came to be *above* the hospital, where she saw streets, buildings and the lights of the city. She also told me that she saw different intensities of brightness and wondered if that was what people meant when they referred to colors.

Vicki was only one such case of the congenitally blind who reported some kind of vision during their NDE; as I've mentioned, there were others. How such eyeless vision, which I called mindsight, can occur is something I speculate about in my book, but the fact that it occurs is incontestable, however inexplicable it appears.

What does all this research have to tell us about the kind of body we may find ourselves in after death? Of course, no one can say with certainty, but the implication is that it will be one in which all of the senses we have in our earthly body are somehow able to function with perfect clarity. And if that's so, it stands to reason that whatever infirmities or physical limitations we have here will be absent *there.*

Think of it this way. When we dream, we are usually not aware of any bodily limitations. Indeed, we may not even be aware of having a "dream body." I know that in my own dreams, I am aware of myself, but not my body. Now, don't misunderstand: An NDE is in no way like a dream; it is far more real. From the standpoint of an NDE, it is *more* real than what we call life, and certainly more real than even the most vivid dream. Nevertheless, our dreams are perhaps the best intimation of the wonders that await us after we die. And in that state, the one that we can anticipate when we die, all bodily malfunctions appear to be transcended.

When I contemplate such possibilities, I know it makes it a lot easier for me to deal with the signs of my own creeping decrepitude and my increasingly poor vision. I know that they are only the temporary impediments of my aging body.

In any case, you can now understand that I am not just waiting to die. I'm waiting to *see*. Perfectly.

CHAPTER THIRTEEN

Kenneth Letterman

These days as I cope with a condition I have sorrowfully come to realize is one from which I shall never recover—I am referring to old age, which I don't recommend (though I am still searching for a reverse gear on eBay)—I have come to realize that I am also living on a kind of island. Around me are the waters of my own incapacity comprised of all the things I used to enjoy doing or at least *could* do that are now off-limits to me. Mostly the terra firma of my daily life is located in my own home and the nearby bike path where I still occasionally saunter, sometimes with a tread of steely determination, though more often with a sullen trudge.

Even at home, where on occasion of an evening I entertain myself with a movie on streaming video (praise be to Netflix and Amazon Prime), I am reminded of my island. For example, when I see a film that is situated in a city abroad, I am aware that I will never see one again and even if I could travel there, I couldn't deal with the crowds and the hurly-burly of swarms of pedestrians. And with my poor vision, I would be a candidate for my instant demise if I were ever able to attempt to cross a busy intersection. Can you imagine me trying to traverse the streets circling the Arch of Triumph on the Champs-Élysées? Monsieur Magoo would soon be a pancake.

Most men my age, or at any age, might amuse themselves with a hobby of some sort—woodworking, golf, having a clandestine love affair, etc., but being Jewish I have never been clever with my hands. You know what they say about Jews—they only use their hands to point. So much for being Homo faber—man the maker. Tools and I have always been strangers to each other; with Thomas Carlyle, I find them completely alien and manifestly dangerous. There must be some kind of psychiatric term for an unreasoning phobia of tools. Whatever it is, I have a bad, incurable case of it. Some people fear spiders or heights; I become frightened whenever I see someone using an electric saw.

Maybe it's because I am descended from a long line of Lithuanian rabbis (that is actually true, and it makes a great excuse). These were men who spent their lives obsessively reading Torah and Talmud, and never lifting a finger while their wives ran the business, raised and scolded the kids, and shushed them when the great man was trying to study. Even my Aunt Mary, who was really my mother in many ways, would shoo her husband away from my bedroom, whispering, " Be quiet, George; Kenny is studying."

Of course, by the time I was a young teenager, I found that I could actually use my hand for various purposes, including that of auto-eroticism, which although I was no Portnoy, I decided would be good to cultivate. (Girls came later, and there I could use both hands.) But eventually, I found what my hands were really suited for, and this was just about the only thing that has lasted: writing. So what if I couldn't be a member of the species, Homo faber. I had found my own species where I belonged: Homo sematicus.

So I became a professor and learned to write for a living. And after having written nearly a score of books and maybe a hundred articles or so, I looked at my still serviceable hands and asked them, "what now, old friends?" They considered the matter and eventually they had an answer for me.

"Write letters," they said.

So, thanks for the mixed blessings of e-mail, that's what I've been doing while remaining on my island waiting to die. It's just me and my trusty desktop iMac. I am passing the time by writing to my friends as well as to various professionals who find their way to my inbox. It's one of the few things I can still do, and I expect to keep writing, even on my deathbed. William Blake sang on his; I hope to be tapping on my keyboard until I croak.

So here are some samples from my life as Kenneth Letterman.

Lately, I've been writing to a new friend who turns out to be a farmer on the East Coast. I don't have much experience with farmers, and the last time I can remember being on a farm was when I was fourteen and working on a peach farm in central California, illegally, to be sure. I remember my foreman telling me in pretty much these words, speaking of the "winos" (as they were called in those days), "Well, kid, now you'll see how the other half live." I was not sure I wanted to know. Fortunately, my boyhood buddy, Lorry, who was sharing this illicit adventure with me, soon developed a nosebleed after which there was an earthquake, after which my parents and Lorry's decided they had better rescue us before something worse happened.

So I wrote to my new friend:

> *Of course, we Jews were mostly not allowed to farm, so we became urban people and specialized in growing money. (Unfortunately, I never got the gene for the latter.) I think I've been on a farm once or twice, and found it completely alien to my spirit and smelling of manure. On this score, I'm with Woody Allen who said "nature and I are two."*

I have another friend (I actually have perhaps five or six friends at last count) whom I'll call Jack. Jack's about my age and lives up in Oregon where he manages an apartment complex. He is one of my few — or perhaps my only — gay friends. He is also the funniest man I know — his letters, which usually come once a year around the time of my birthday, when he also sends me very thoughtful presents, invariably crack me up. They are side-splitting funny. I have often told him that he missed his calling by not becoming a stand-up comedian to which he usually retorts with a quip to the effect that these days, he can no longer stand up at all, and even has to squat to urinate. And that's no joking matter, he will add.

I first got acquainted with Jack when I was living back in

Connecticut and still active as an NDE researcher. At that time, I was considering undertaking a research project having to do with NDEs among gays, and I as I recall somehow I was put in touch with Jack in that connection. That research never got very far, but Jack and I became devoted friends in the course of our correspondence. He was also very interested in NDEs and spiritual matters, and we had a lot of deep discussions about those topics in our letters, which were fairly frequent in those years.

After I moved to California, Jack was finally able to come to visit me here (he arrived with "a rent boy"), and we had a bang-up time together. If I were able to turn gay, Jack would be my kind of guy. Despite meeting only that one time, I regard Jack as one of my most precious friends. His letters to me are not only hilarious and clever, but full of expressions of appreciation — and almost reverence — for me. How can you not love a guy like that?

These days, we also write about what we are reading, often talk about mathematics (I am keen to read about mathematicians, even though my mathematical ability is roughly that of an ape), and of course as befits old men, about our ailments.

Here's just one of my letters to Jack I wrote a couple of years ago, just to give you a feeling for the pleasures his letters always give me.

> *I can always count on you for the veritable "barrel full of laughs" whenever I receive a letter from you. I know I've said that you missed your calling by not being a stand-up comedian, but since you seem to spend most of your life sitting on your local commode these days (and nights), maybe you should consider just becoming a sit-down comedian and save your feet for break dancing. On the other hand, I remember learning from the film, "My Favorite Year," starring the ever-dazzling Peter O'Toole, that one should never tell a joke sitting down. Just why that was, was never made clear. There's also a really funny scene in that film when Peter O'Toole is*

swinging like Tarzan on a rope just before he is to land on stage and shouts to contradict an admirer, "I'm not an actor, I'm a movie star!" Well, maybe you had to be there. I suggest you go directly to Netflix, order the damn film, and watch that scene. Then you'll be able to laugh.

But as we are old and doddery, not to say dingy, why shouldn't we dwell on our urinary trials? Some of my greatest recent adventures have had me diving into ditches by the roadside on trips down the coast when a toilet wasn't handy. Passing motorists would toot me on as I dribbled urine down my pant leg. And going to the toilet only two or three times a night would be a good night for me, Jack. Just wait until you reach my age as you approach what I am pleased to call "advanced middle age."

Your Retirement—Who Cares? clock and I are still ticking away, though I seem to be ticking at a somewhat slower rate these days, as befits an aging though newly minted octogenarian. And aren't you (characteristically) clever to find such a wonderful mathematical way to express my age. Here I had been content merely to say that I was now 9 squared minus one (I wish I knew how to create numerical superscripts on this computer, but it is clearly just another one of my 613 failings, the exact number of laws that an Orthodox Jew needs to obey in order to bring down another messiah into our midst, who is unlikely to prosper any better than the last one). Anyway, I was charmed to get a birthday greeting from you again this year, and by sending it late you actually didn't have to contend with the crowd, most of whom have now left me in peace or is it pieces? Possibly both.

Actually, I had an early 80th birthday bash in mid-August this year. It was attended by all the members of my less than illustrious family—my three kids, their spouses, and all five of my grandchildren—the first time that my entire family had been assembled in one place, ever! And of course it was supplemented by a motley assortment of my ne'er-do-well friends who pretended to admire me exceedingly. No, really, I had a great time getting roasted, toasted and embarrassingly drunk, and they tell me I had the time of my life, though frankly I can't remember anything that happened after I started to eat that spiked chocolate cake.

Now for true confessions. (Is there any other kind?) I have already read quite a bit about this mathematical wunderkind, Ramanujan, and his relationship with Hardy (though I never knew Hardy was gay—leave it to you to know such arcana), but Jack, my vision is now so bad that I simply can't deal with that tiny Tim font. I'm almost blind as it is and this book, were I actually to try to read it, would certainly render me Samson-like without the muscles. Besides, it is too technical for a mathematical doofus like me. I really prefer my mathematicians without the math, to be honest. But if it's the thought that counts, even if I can't count beyond my finger limits, it was a hit. Still, would you like me to return it so that you can give it to someone who actually has 20-10 vision and a thing for Indian mathematicians, whether they be gay or not?

But, don't worry, Jack. That doesn't mean I am going to return your presents or send back that raucous birthday card. On the contrary, I've found the perfect place for that hilarious "retirement clock" of yours—no, not in my toilet—and will also look forward to reading that humorous book you sent me, assuming my eyes last that long. Anyway, your antic gifts were much appreciated.

Otherwise, just to re-assure you, except for not being able to see, always asking people, "what was that you just said?", having more false teeth than ever, living on smoothies, and not being able to travel, life is peachy keen.

And with that, along with your other assignment from the Netflix archives, I will mercifully release you to

other pleasures, not excluding those of the urinary kind,
of course.

Take care of those eyes of yours, Jack, and your other
body parts. And thanks again for making me a happy
Ken, as I always am when I hear from you.

My friend Jan, a Norwegian playwright and author, and I met
in the mid-eighties in California when we were both interested
to pursue an amatory relationship with a woman named Leah
who introduced us. We met in a little restaurant in Storrs, where
the University of Connecticut is located, and I was immediately
smitten — with Jan (who got and married the girl). He was culti-
vated, with the kind of courtly charm that only Europeans appear
to have, was very literate, and interested in many of the same
subjects — NDEs, psychedelics, consciousness studies — in
which I was then absorbed. We became friends almost immediately — friendship at first sight, one might say — and have
remained the best of friends ever since.

After that first meeting, we managed to see each other frequently. He lived for a while in the States with Leah, so I saw him
frequently during those years. But after they divorced, I visited
him many times (five altogether) in Norway, and also spent some
time traveling with him and my fourth wife, Barbara, in Italy,
where we spent three weeks together one winter. In those days, I
was using psychedelics and taking Ecstasy, and as Jan was, too,
we sometimes took our journeys together.

Both Jan and I have had many lovers and each us of has
been married four times. During the '80s and '90s, we were both
involved in a series of romantic ventures, so that when we got
together, we would usually spend a lot of time ruing some of the
unwise decisions we had made — or were still making! — in our
love lives. During those years, Jan became my dearest friend and
male confidant.

But after our lives settled down — Jan has now been married
for a long time to his Norwegian wife Astrid — and we became
older, it was more difficult to arrange to see each other, so we

naturally started to write to each other, and we continue to do so fairly frequently to this day.

Jan is now 92, and is still active writing his plays (three in the last two years!) and reading. These days, we mostly write about what we are reading when we are not discussing our most recent health trials. (Jan has had to have a pacemaker implanted and also suffers chronic pain from spinal stenosis, of which I have a mild case myself.). But mostly it's "the reading life" that occupies our attention.

Although I've just heard from Jan, who is still dong well, here's one of my typical letters I wrote to him just when it was clear that Donald Trump would receive the nomination for president.

Always happy to hear from you, mon frère, and glad that you enjoyed reading Augustus. Before I started that book, I had read a long narrative history called Dynasty about the first five emperors of Rome, and by far the longest section dealt with Octavius/Augustus. From reading that account of his life, I could tell that Williams had been pretty faithful in his depiction of Augustus, but of course he used his skill as a novelist to blend history with plausible invention. I found the book very compelling.

Meanwhile, I just started another book, and a classic, about a famous Roman emperor of a different era, Hadrian. The book is called Memoirs of Hadrian and it may well have inspired Williams to write his book for all I know.

Here, for what it's worth, is a brief summary of the other books I am currently reading.

I may be straighter than a Euclidian line, but I seem to be fascinated to read about gay life. Right now, I'm reading a book called Homintern: How Gay Culture Liberated the Modern World. It basically tells the story of the rise and dominance of gay culture beginning with Oscar Wilde. I have already spent a lot of time in the gay subculture of Russian ballet (mostly in France, actually), in Paris, especially in the period between the wars, and Berlin during the Weimar Republic. I'm convinced that every important artist was either gay or bi-sexual. Heterosexuals like me are dull fare compared to the people I've been reading about. I have obviously missed out on a lot, Jan. Anyway, I recommend the book if you are at all interested in this sort of thing—it's well written, not gossipy, but the author, a poet himself, seems to be familiar with every gay liaison that ever was.

Another book that I've been listening to (Lauren has been reading it to me) is a counter-factual novel by Philip Roth called The Plot Against America. It imagines what life in America would have been like for Jews had Charles Lindbergh, a well-known Nazi sympathizer, been elected President after which Hitler wins the war. The book has very clear resonances to what's going on in America today with the rise of our next President, Donald J. Trump, who just last night received the nomination by the Republican Party, which has clearly taken a Trumpian turn toward a kind of Mussolini-like fascism. The only good news about this is that I will soon be moving to Norway. Do you think you can put me up for a few days until I can get settled there?

Finally, I have a book to recommend to you, even though it's not fiction. Check out When Breath Becomes Air by Paul Kalanithi on Amazon. It's extremely moving and, again, beautifully written. It deservedly was the number one bestseller on The New York Times Booklist. You won't be disappointed.

Oh, wait. I just remembered a wrote a brief review of it for Amazon. I'll paste it in here....

When Breath Becomes Air is easily the best book I've read in the last year. The man who wrote it, a neurosurgeon at Stanford named Paul Kalanithi, died just about a year ago on March 20th. In his book, he tells the story of his life and of his (facing) death. He has written a poem. A brave man, rigorously honest, deeply feeling, and a literary man to his core, who was also a dedicated and highly honored neurosurgeon, he has written a book of searing beauty and unsparing self-revelation about what it's like to die. It has quickly and deservedly become a bestseller. His wife, Lucy, contributed a very affecting epilogue that almost made me cry. Paul died of lung cancer at thirty-seven and received many moving eulogies from his friends, family and colleagues. This book completes his life and gives it its ultimate meaning. His writing is a source of joy, which is only one of the many gifts to be derived from this jewel of a book.

Well, that should keep you busy for a while, mon vieux. In the meantime, keep writing those plays, keep writing to me and please tell Astrid to prepare a bed for me. I'll be arriving soon.

Like me, most of my friends now are old, and quite a few of them with whom I enjoyed lively e-mail exchanges have gone on to better things. Ultimately, we old guys find ourselves not only with diminishing resources but subject to becoming a kind of amity-based orphan, abandoned by friends and stuck on a small island while the wider world whirls on without us (how's that for an alliterative riff?). Still, it's not bad. As long as my fingers still work and a few friends remain—and the electricity stays on—you will find me happily typing away on my little island writing my letters and, when my hands are quiet, dreaming of the life I once had and yearning for the life to come, still waiting to die.

CHAPTER FOURTEEN

La Famiglia e gli altri
sulla strada verso la morte

All right, yes, I am in an Italian mode today. I'm afraid you'll have to deal with it, even if not for long (though you may have to put up with me longer). Besides, it's good to stretch your brain every once in a while, and at this point in my life, it's about the only part of my body I can stretch without it hurting. In any event, if you're not up to doing the translation, you'll see soon enough where this is heading. Right now, it's to my mother who was not Italian, though when she was young she was as beautiful as a madonna in a painting by Raphael.

However, by the time she was close to the end, her beauty had long been gone and she was eager to get on with it. At that point, I thought I might be of some help to her, but as you'll see, I was left only with a rueful smile after my mother responded to my offer to advise her about what she would be in for when she died.

My mother had a sad life and a long and slow descent toward the edge of the cliff of her death over which she toppled at the age of almost 89 in June of 2001. Her last years were spent in a nursing home in Berkeley where, until her last year or so, I was accustomed to pushing her around the neighborhood in her wheelchair. She was, however, lucid to the end, even though she was by then hard of hearing and generally very passive. She did not like to be touched, and mostly she was taciturn, too. I tried to entertain her by recounting my latest adventures and sharing family news.

"You talk too much," she said to me one day.

On another occasion, when I thought she might not have long to live, I spent five minutes or so telling her about my work on near-death experiences. Finally, I asked her, "So, mom, what do you expect will happen when you die?"

She narrowed her eyes and replied in a flat voice: "Nothing. I expect to be dead."

Once, on what turned out to be one of our last times together, I asked her if she could tell me some of the things in her life that had given her the most happiness.

"You," she said.

I found myself thinking of my mother today when I was trudging on a dirt path along the creek that runs in my neighborhood on my way to my local bookstore to pick up some sustenance for what's left of my brain. Lately, I have been having a helluva time walking, and this short journey to the bookstore, which I used to traverse easily without thinking, has become, if not an arduous undertaking, at least one that requires more effort on my part than I had been accustomed to for so many years. It was as if what had been a flat path had suddenly become a sharp incline.

What made me think of my mother was that in her last years she had developed what I was told were "contractures" in her legs, so that she was no longer able to walk at all—hence her wheelchair. Since I am now only a few years from the age my mother died, it occurred to me that perhaps my walking days might also be on a short leash. It could be that I will become one of those old duffers who scoot around in one of those motorized chairs, zipping along the sidewalks, frightening dogs and terrorizing old ladies carrying their groceries home from the market.

Even now, however, I make a pretty pitiful sight ambling down the avenue, listing to my left from my scoliosis and bent over as if I am searching for a precious lost coin. Now that my vision at least has improved somewhat, thanks to my finding a competent optometrist recently, I may have to relinquish my self-appointed title as Mr. Magoo of Marin, only to be dubbed the halt alter cocker of Kentfield. (As you can see, my linguistic versatility enables me to switch easily from Italian to Yiddish.)

Whether I will share my mother's fate about the use of my legs is uncertain, but of course I know that I will be sharing her ultimate fate when the state of my legs will no longer be of concern. Actually, I don't have much a family left at all to accompany me on the road toward death. I am now twice the age of my father when he died, so both my parents are naturally long gone. I am one of four male cousins. My cousin, Roger, a podiatrist who attained fame (or perhaps notoriety) in his final years as a UFO researcher, died a few years ago at 79. Not long afterward, my cousin Don, an internationally renowned jazz pianist, succumbed to cancer at 81. Now only my cardiologist cousin, Cliff, who is really like a brother to me and who is close to 80 himself, is left of that original quarter, along with me. I am now the eldest as I head for the unchartered territory of 83. Like many people of this vintage, I'm sure, I wonder what I'm doing here; I never expected or wanted to live this long.

To be sure, I have my children, and that is certainly a boon to me as I venture ever closer to my dotage, but here I am thinking about my contemporaries who are gradually sliding down the embankments of the road toward death that I have been treading along, however lamely, for a while now.

There's that old song, "You'll never walk alone," from the Rodgers and Hammerstein musical *Carousel*, but as you walk along that final road, while you may never be alone, the ranks of your friends and family gradually thin out, so that waiting to die is always punctuated by loss and sadness. My knowledge of NDEs, frankly, does not help me much to assuage the loss of irreplaceable family members and dear friends.

One of those dear friends who recently died was a Dutch NDEr with the unusual name of Joke (pronounced "Yoka), short for Joanna. I first met her about twenty-five years ago on my first trip to Amsterdam. Quite by chance, at the last moment, one night she impulsively invited some friends and me to her apartment after dinner, and I still remember how astonished I was to find it lined with thousands of books, from top to bottom, along all of its walls. I was immediately enraptured; I felt that I could be very happy there for months exploring her many books— notwithstanding the fact, of course, that most of them were not in English. But what happened next was really what bonded Joke and me for life, as it turned out. While others were talking, she was speaking to me and happened to put on a recording of Fritz Wunderlich singing Tamino's aria from The Magic Flute. I happened to love Fritz Wunderlich (as did Joke) and recognized his voice immediately. The rest of the evening was passed in a mood of enchantment; I have never forgotten it.

Joke and I stayed in touch ever after, and we saw each other again, too, both in Amsterdam and here in California.

But you know what I particularly remember about that trip here? It may surprise you; it certainly did me. She loved to shop, so we went shopping together. She tried on clothes and I either nodded or shook my head. We had a ball together.

Otherwise, we maintained contact over the years by e-mail. She would write me funny letters in her quixotic English, and some that were not so funny, but more serious, as when she was having troubles, either physically or emotionally. But I was always happy to see her name in my inbox.

I kept in touch with her until almost the very end when she was no longer able to write. She would sometimes ask me to send her jokes, which I did. I was happy to give her something to make her laugh while she still could.

In just about her last note to me she wrote:

"I would like to stay in a beautiful hotel and look at the blue sea. And I would like to talk with you and go shopping with you one more time...

I live day by day now. Have no idea how long this will last. This life as Joke.

Please keep sending your thoughts.

I love you."

As I write, I look off to my right, and a few feet away me, on the wall of my study, is a large framed color photograph. In the background, we see Patmos on a sparkling clear day, with the cerulean waters of the Aegean Sea providing more atmospheric beauty to the scene. In the foreground, there is a woman seated on a white ledge who is holding aloft in her right hand a bouquet of white flowers. On her face is a smile that radiates pure joy.

It is of course a photograph of Joke—Joke on her wedding day about ten years ago. Beside her stands her husband, Robert, in a dark suit, much older than his beautiful wife, with his shock of white hair. I can't tell if he is looking bemused or perplexed or simply with indulgent affection at his new bride.

This has always been my favorite photo—of many that I have—of Joke. It expresses so well *her joie de vivre* as well as the beauty of her spirit. It has been my daily companion for years now, and it will continue to remain on my wall as long as I am here. My knowledge of NDEs may not help me when I mourn the death of close friends, but this photograph of Joke does, especially now.

But as a kind of compensation for these losses, and to remind me that the road toward death may also have its unexpected rewards, some recent encounters have certainly served to lift my spirits and helped to banish these gloomy reflections. More new people are coming into my life now, seemingly to make up for the ones I have lost. And not a few of them have come my way as a result of reading these little essays of mine on the University of Heaven website. Here I'd like to share just a little bit about two of them, who have already become new and valued friends of mine.

First, not long ago I received a letter from an NDEr who had attended one of my workshops in Massachusetts in the mid-1980s. I had not heard from her in all these years until I received this letter out of the blue. It went on for four pages, but here are just the first few paragraphs. You can imagine how it bucked up my spirits to read it.

Dear Dr Funny or, should I say, Dear Dr Clever....
Whatever might prove more apropos. I must begin
by sharing what a good giggle I got from your rendition

of the arduous challenges of an aging body. Your light touch has proven to be a helpful counterbalance to my own daily challenges of pain and stiffness. Clearly, I'm not as philosophical nor am I as sanguine as you seem to be. I regard my morning misery as a thief of time robbing an hour or more each day before my brain clears and my body moves without clenched teeth and considerable grumbling and fear of crushing the cat. Please tell me this fate of creeping senescence doesn't inflict every oldster as it does us. That's quite a horrible vision to have in one's head. Thanks for lightening my load, and my groaning revolt with your delightful humor.

I also want to thank you for your kind and enthusiastic response to my email about NDE. When reading your books through the years, I have always been deeply impressed by what I sensed to be your genuine warmth and true appreciation to those who write to you. I must add that it is my observation that these qualities are unique to you. None of the other NDE researchers project the kindness, appreciation and genuine affability with which you "ring" so true.

More words of gratitude coming your way... This time for the manner in which your writing, especially Omega, provided a map of the realm of life after NDE. I may have never found my way had it not been for what, I assume, may have been a bit of risky business when you conjectured about the evolutionary path of Mother Kundalini...

Then there is a woman I'll call Florence who also had been familiar with my work and books on NDEs, and was full of praise for them, which naturally caused me immediately to go out and buy a new hat for my now somewhat inflated head. But it quickly turned out that Florence wanted to write to me about an important new discovery she had made (that I am not at liberty to disclose) that could lead to important advances in anti-aging research. The strange thing about this discovery, however, was that it also had implications for NDEs, so Florence was writing to me about a research project she had in mind involving out-of-body experiences (OBEs) and evidence for the subtle luminous body that is often referred to in the esoteric tradition.

I was instantly fascinated.

However, at the time, as usual, I was also then preoccupied with a number of my painful bodily infirmities, and happened to allude briefly to these annoying distractions in one of my early letters to Florence. She immediately wrote back a long letter with a number of specific suggestions for remedies, most of which I had never heard of, but some of which I was persuaded to try (and they did help). But what particularly struck me about Florence's letters over the next week or so was how deeply knowledgeable she was about these matters, so much so that she soon had become something like my health guru and was offering to share her knowledge on all sorts of treatments that would help to make me well. She seemed to take a personal interest in extending my life and nurturing me back to health, which certainly was at odds and threatened to interfere with my "waiting to die" orientation.

But what impressed me even more forcibly was Florence's constant compassionate solicitude for my welfare; I was very touched by and grateful for her dedication to my well being.

Our letters, which were now nearly daily exchanges, were about more than the trials of my body, however. Eventually, Florence started to write to me about some of the ancient authorities on death—mostly Greek and Neo-Platonist philosphers, who often wrote about the Eleusinian Mysteries of ancient Greece and whose writings clearly anticipated the findings of modern NDE research.

As it happens, I had written some articles on this same subject many years ago and was familiar with most of the writers Florence cited. But what knocked me out was the specific quotations Florence was able to cite, which I had long forgotten, whose relevance to NDE findings she was keen to remind me of. To give you a sense of what Florence, who now gave me the impression of being a classical scholar, was then sharing with me, let me simply quote some extracts from one of her letters:

I have no doubt that you are right when comparing the Mysteries rites to achieving the NDE.

Plutarch considered people who did not understand these things as being deprived (according to comments attributed to Plutarch in a fifth century A.D. compilation by Joannes Stobaeus), evidenced by his remarks when comparing the release of the soul during Mystery rites to what was believed to occur at death:

"When a man dies, he is like those who are being initiated into the mysteries...Our whole life is but a succession of wanderings, of painful courses, of long journeys by tortuous ways without outlet. At the moment of quitting it, fears, terrors, quiverings, mortal sweats, and a lethargic stupor, cover over us and overwhelm us; but as soon as we are out of it, pure spots and meadows receive us, with voices and dances and the solemnities of sacred words and holy sights. It is there that man, having become perfect and initiated—restored in liberty really master of himself—celebrates, crowned with myrtle, the most august mysteries, holds converse with just and pure souls, looking down upon the impure multitude of the profane or uninitiated, sinking in the mire and mist beneath him—through fear of death and through disbelief in the life to come, abiding in its miseries."

We can check this against Porphyrus, who put things this way (for those who reached the épopteia during the Eleusinian Mysteries): "Then, finally, the light of a serene wonder fills the temple; we see the pure fields of Elysium; we hear the chorus of the blessed..."

Proclus said this about the Eleusinian Mysteries (and, like Porphyrus, he appears to be talking about those who reach the highest stage so that they see the Divine Light): "The soul also, beholding that which is arcane shining forth as it were to the view, rejoices in, and admires that which it sees, and is astonished about it."

You are, of course, also right about Lessons from the

Light—and Diodorus would cheer you on. Speaking of the Samothracian Mysteries, he wrote (Diodorus, Library of History 49.1-6, Loeb tr.):

"The claim is also made that men who have taken part in the mysteries become more pious and more just and better in every respect than they were before."

I think this is a mystery to be clinically studied and duplicated because these lessons might be the only thing that can change the hearts of those who war monger for profit or sit on billions while ignoring the poverty stricken of this world.

But the most astonishing revelation of the range of Florence's accomplishments was yet to come. She was not, she insisted, a classical scholar of the sort I had imagined. Not at all. What she is was the woman who had helped to promote an ingenious theory of how the Egyptian pyramids had been built! Indeed, she had developed and made the case for an interpretation that had originally been advanced by the man for whom she had worked for many years to whom she gives all credit—years when she seems to have spent much of her life crawling all over the great Pyramid at Giza until she knew every limestone intimately. She eventually had written a highly praised book about this discovery—which I then started to read and was bowled over by—and was often cited for her groundbreaking research on this subject.

Once she had made me aware of her writings and work on this subject, and I had got over being thoroughly dazzled by it, I could now understand more about this extraordinary woman who had entered into my life. Though her excessive modesty would surely take issue with my impressions of her, to me she was clearly an autodidact, a polymath, and a certifiable genius. In helping us to understand how the Egyptians had built the first Wonder of the Ancient World, I could see that Florence was, as it were, at least to me, the eighth Wonder of the Modern World. She was a treasure, and had certainly become more than that to me. I began to think that maybe she was a lifesaver, too.

Her serendipitous entrance into my life—along with several other new people I don't have the space to mention here who have also brought excitement and stimulation to me recently—has got me thinking that maybe I need to reconsider my waiting to die conceit that has been the theme of these essays. Maybe it's really that I am just entering another stage of my life *before* my death. Maybe I will be around for longer than I had supposed. Who knows?

So now I think—so what if I can only stumble around my town like the decrepit hunchback of Norte California on legs as wobbly as an unbalanced kitchen table? As long as I can let my fingers do the walking over the non-noisy keys of my computer and as long as I have people like Florence and others to both entertain and thrill me, I'm inclined to hang on for another round. Who knows who will next show up in my inbox to intrigue and delight me? Hey, maybe it'll be you!

CHAPTER FIFTEEN

Eighty-Three and Counting

It is good to have an end to journey toward;
but it is the journey that matters, in the end.

—URSULA K. LE GUIN

I've just turned eighty-three. Of course, I'd prefer to turn back, but so far I haven't been able to locate a reverse gear. Still, I must confess I had a good time this year. My birthday actually has become something of a national holiday over the years and goes on for well over a week during which time I enjoy receiving greetings from near and far from my misguided friends, family and a stray fan or two. And then there are various celebratory lunches with local friends and more and diverse pleasures with my girlfriend, Lauren, the nature of which my innate modesty precludes me from disclosing. Well, I could go on, but then I'm sure you would justifiably accuse me of an undue level of rodomontade.

Now if can manage to live to be 1000 months old, I'll be 83 and 1/3. A good time to die. And did you know that the hero of my admittedly callow youth, Sigmund Freud, also died at 83 & 1/3—and at exactly 1000 months. You could look it up. Hey, I'd be in pretty stellar company, right?

And look at some of the other famous people who died at 83.

David Lean
Lord Alfred Tennyson
Edgar Degas

Gene Wilder
Thomas Jefferson
Victor Hugo
Gene Kelly
Paul Newman
Henry Ford
Samuel Beckett
Ted Williams
Leonard Nimoy
Andrew Carnegie

I sure wouldn't mind joining that 83 club, even if I lack any celebrity credentials of my own, though I can always hope to achieve some measure of posthumous fame if ever a good biographer comes along to extol my virtues and conceal my sins.

Actually, not long ago, just as I was approaching 83, I had a near-death scare because if I believed the rumors that were circulating about me for a couple of days then, I seemed to have died already.

I had no idea about the rumors swirling about concerning my alleged death until I received a call from a longtime NDE colleague of mine who NEVER calls me. When I heard his emotional voice on the phone, I thought he was calling me to tell me that someone in the NDE community had died. I had no clue that that someone seemed to be me!

When I picked up the phone, I heard my friend gasp and then say, "Oh, Ken, you're alive!"

"Of course, I'm alive, you silly goose. Just because I've been writing all these essays about waiting to die doesn't mean I've actually caught the disease." (I am paraphrasing and exaggerating a bit here for dramatic effect. Am I having any?)

My friend said that a near-death experiencer (NDEr) of our acquaintance had been spreading the good news. It made me wonder why she didn't call me first.

As soon as I hung up, the phone rang again. This time the incoming President of IANDS, the NDE organization I had co-founded in 1981, was on the line. Another version of the same conversion took place. Egad, what next?

Shortly afterward, I was able to piece together how this rumor got started. Do you remember in one of my earlier essays called "Cheers at the Half," I had mentioned a letter from a longtime NDE friend and author which she had entitled "Remembering Ken Ring?" At the time, I joked that it made me think I was reading my own eulogy.

Well, recently, that letter was published in Vital Signs, the quarterly newsletter of IANDS, and the NDEr I mentioned apparently read it as if it were entitled "In Remembrance of Ken Ring," so naturally she thought I had left the building—for good (*pace* Frasier). At that point she got in touch with the woman who had written that article who, having no reason to doubt the NDEr, put out an announcement about my purported death of her website. Why *she* didn't check in me with first, God knows?

Well, you can imagine the next two days, putting those rumors to rest that I had not been laid to rest. Apologies were extended, laughs were exchanged, and I got back to merely writing about waiting to die again and was spared from the formality of its actually occurring.

Not long after this faux near-death episode, I wondered into my local bookstore looking for a new novel. And guess what immediately caught my eye? A book by the title of *The Secret Diary of Hendrik Groen,* but it was the full title that told me this was the book I was meant to read at this time.

The Secret Diary of
HENDRIK GROEN
83 1/4 Years Old

And this Dutchman, my exact contemporary, turned out to be an octogenarian after my own heart and, if I may say so, in my own moldy mold. Like me, he has found that humor is what gets him through his day as he deals with the kind of decrepitude that I have often bemoaned in these essays. His piquant sense of humor is delightful as this passage will demonstrate. Does Hendrik remind you of anyone you know?

> My "dribbling" keeps getting worse. White underpants are excellent for highlighting yellow stains. Yellow underpants would be a lot better. I'm mortified at the thought of the laundry ladies handling my soiled garments. [Hendrik lives in an assisted living home in Amsterdam.] I have therefore taken to scrubbing the worst stains by hand before sending the washing out. Call it a pre-prewash. If I didn't send out anything to be laundered it would arouse suspicion. "You have been changing your underwear, haven't you, Mr. Groen?" the fat lady from housekeeping would probably ask. What I'd like to reply is, "No, fat lady from housekeeping, this pair is caked so firmly onto the old buttocks that I think I'll just keep wearing them for the rest of my days."

> It has been a trying day: the body creaks in all its joints. There's nothing that will stop the decline. Hair is not going to grow back. (Not on the pate at least; it readily sprouts from the nose and ears...) and the leaking nether parts aren't going to stop dripping.

I can't seem to get away from tales of urinary distress so reminiscent of my own, especially those that I alluded to in my very first essay.

For example, during the last couple of weeks, my girlfriend Lauren and I have been watching a very popular comedy on Netflix called The Kominksy Method. It's stars a 74-year-old Michael Douglas as a theater coach (since his career as a leading actor—at least in this series—is washed up) and Alan Arkin, who is ten years older and Douglas's former agent, as his best friend. Arkin, whose beloved wife has just died, is the archetypal curmudgeon while Douglas, with his grizzled beard and cool leather jacket, still is trying to cozy up to women, oozing the last drop of his fading charm.

Unfortunately, that's not all he's oozing.

In the third episode, Douglas begins to have prostate problems and is always having to go to the bathroom, at the most embarrassing times, so that everyone becomes well aware of his urinary exigencies. One night, he is saying goodnight to his girlfriend—one of his drama students—outside her house. They kiss, and he starts leaving when he stops and says "uh-oh." He looks around furtively, sees that no one is watching, and then pees in her bushes as a sigh of relief washes over his face.

The story of my life! I have been there, believe me, and worse! Did he have to remind me?

Eventually, Douglas has to visit a urologist who is played by the hilarious Danny DeVito Any man of a certain age, and I am of that age, will relate to the examination that DeVito then performs. I squirmed throughout that scene while my girlfriend, of course, found it uproarious.

I do recommend the show, however, particularly to men under the age of thirty.

Seriously, however, it does depict, both with humor and with a certain pathos, the trials of old men like me, especially Arkin, who is about my age, and in the series is clearly waiting to die.

Before I leave this bathroom humor behind, I have to confess that I still find that when I piss, I often continue to get a secondary stream that runs down my left leg. That really pisses me off. Sometimes it happens twice in a row. What do you think I say then?

Another double dribble.

I'm winding up talking about the same things I mentioned at the beginning of these essays. I'm not progressing toward death; I'm going in circles!

One day long ago I had a shocking realization. I received a new credit card whose expiration date was November, 2023, when I would be almost 87 years old. Surely, I thought, I would expire long before that. But, then, a horrible thought occurred to me: What if I don't?! What if I live to 86? Honestly, before seeing that card, I had never imagined such a thing. No, no! Will I still be walking on this road toward death, still waiting to die, for years to come? What a ghastly thought.

I realized I'm not afraid to die; I'm now afraid of living too long!

Meanwhile, I seem to have reached the end of this stage of my journey toward death, if not the end of the road—but the road stretches on. I am still shooting for 1000 months. If I get there, I may possibly shoot myself since I think it would be keen-o to go out with a bang (get it?) on such a splendid number. [Just kidding, don't worry. Not being a rabid gun-toting member of the NRA, I have never even touched a firearm. I don't even know anyone who has one, and I don't think I'd like to, thank you.]

I will now take leave of you by recalling the lyrics of a song from Carousel, the musical by Richard Rodgers and Oscar Hammerstein. In light of these essays dealing with NDEs, try reading these lyrics as a metaphor for life's journey on the road toward death and what you will experience on the way:

>When you walk through a storm
>Hold your head up high
>And don't be afraid of the dark
>At the end of a storm
>There's a golden sky
>And the sweet silver song of a lark
>Walk on through the wind
>Walk on through the rain
>Though your dreams be tossed and blown
>Walk on, walk on
>With hope in your heart
>And you'll never walk alone
>You'll never walk alone

On the road toward an infinite journey with Lauren by my side.

Sorry to disappoint you. I'm sure you expected a dramatic finish with me in the hospital, tethered to tubes, surrounded by my relatives some of whom surely wondering if they had been mentioned in my will, and me about to expire.

But *la morte, come la donna, è mobile.* Death is fickle. It comes when it pleases. It has no respect for the contrivance of literary endings. I am not in a Chekhov play after all.

If you want to find out if I made it to my 1000 month goal, turn the page. If it's blank—well, draw your own conclusion! This is mine.

CHAPTER SIXTEEN

1000

Still waiting . . .

Made in the USA
Coppell, TX
15 September 2020